A S
UNT

A STORY
UNTOLD

—————————— *Memoir* ——————————

Anamika

www.whitefalconpublishing.com

A Story Untold

Anamika

www.whitefalconpublishing.com

The contents of this book have been certified and timestamped on
the POA Network blockchain as a permanent proof of existence.
Scan the QR code or visit the URL given on the back cover to
verify the blockchain certification for this book.

The views expressed in this work are solely those of the author
and do not reflect the views of the publisher, and the publisher
hereby disclaims any responsibility for them.

Requests for permission should be addressed to
gera.anamika@gmail.com

ISBN - 978-1-63640-562-9

Fly leaf: To my lifeline "Chikki",
better known as Krish to his friends

Contents

Preface ix

Gratitude... xiii

1. Blessed to be ferried in this charismatic world 1

2. My formative toddler years............................... 10

3. Advancing to a city which had no
    existence on the map... 15

4. Summer vacations and beyond school.............. 28

5. Road to recovery and beyond 40

6. Kalyanam aka Lagna... 52

7. Sibling Bonds 60

8. What works and what does not 66

9. Great blessing of my life from the Almighty...... 72

10. Curtains down 80

11. Redeeming myself 89

12. Exploring and Powering Up...............................98

13. महफ़िल में तेरी हम न रहें जो,
    गम तो नहीं है, गम तो नहीं है।.......................103

14. Having the Thames of my life 108

15. Reflections...112

Preface

"I don't go by the rule book. I lead from the heart, not the head."
— *Diana, Princess of Wales*

The pandemic had hit the world earlier, but it entered our awareness in March 2020. Everyone on the planet was struggling to cope with it, to get accustomed to revised lifestyles which would become the new normal. I was too, as I write this. The news of the pandemic continued to be alarming. We were reeling under social isolation and stress. The Covid time was monotonous, no doubt.

Like others, I felt challenged too. The world seemed to have stopped. I was at home and there was no house-help, no cook, nothing. My ailing Mom had just come from the hospital after a brain stroke. There were three of us in the house —Mom, my son "Chikki" and me. Our dearly loved German Shepherd had passed away on the very day the lockdown was announced in India.

When people who have never had a pet see pet parents mourn the loss of a pet, they probably think it's all an overreaction; after all, it's "just a dog".

However, those who have loved a pet know the truth: Your pet is never "just a pet". The loss can only be understood by animal lovers and no one else. We didn't break the news of his demise to my brothers as both of them were far away. We were devastated and didn't want them to feel helpless. This was our third pet and we have now decided not to have any because of the unbearable pain one has to go through when they pass away. Its just undefinable.

I was doing everything I could to take care of Chikki and Mom. It is said that in old age, your parents are akin to kids. Mom was no exception. She had mood swings which were made worse due to the lockdown. On top of that, my estranged husband "RG", his elder brother and their parents went underground for reasons unknown, at least to us. There have been notices in the newspapers in the 'missing' section but there is still no clue of their whereabouts.

The time seemed distressing, until I thought of doing something different. I discussed with other people to find out what was keeping them going. I saw people posting their transformation videos, culinary skills including the recipe for Dalgona Coffee on social media. Wait, what?? Dalgona Coffee?? Imagine, this item getting a place for itself in the KBC (*Kaun Banega Crorepati*) knock out round. I had to do something which made more sense than to learn about Dalgona Coffee. I decided that like my cohort, I would upskill myself, but differently.

When I had been at work, I had little time for myself because of the ultra-busy schedule as in any other corporate profile. It was always home, family, and work. In a way pandemic provided opportunities, because earlier the time taken up by commuting could now be used constructively, and because of the lockdown, my weekends were also completely free.

I meditated to ask myself what was it that I had wanted to do, apart from my professional career but had to put passion and hobbies on the back burner due to lack of time. I drafted a bucket list of what all I would desire to do in my life. During one such introspection sessions, my thoughts dwelt on what had transpired in my past and after days of brainstorming, I thought to myself, "how about penning down the important incidents of my life? An autobiography may be"?

I took the proposition forward and discussed it with Mom and my brothers. They were thrilled at the idea, and I got an instant go ahead from them. It sounded like a plan, and I was excited beyond words. The best part was that it did not involve moving out of my home or travel, especially during the lockdown.

The first step was to look for a publisher. I zeroed in on White Falcon Publishing. It is a Chandigarh-based publishing house that started operations in 2014. Since then, it has published several bestsellers and award-winning books.

The second step was to create an outline of the book. I got down to defining the chapters, putting the major bullet points of my life's journey. I reflected on my life since birth, the people I had met, the lessons and failures and the journey till now. It took me almost six months to define the layout. Once that was done, the rest fell in place.

Somewhere deep within, I had an inherent desire to share my life's experiences with my readers and how it helped in shaping me into a better person that I am today. My tenacity and persistence kept me on the move and ensured that I never stop or rest, regardless of what may come.

My life has been somewhat unusual with lots of ups and downs. I am happy that I always believed in myself, and I can say with conviction that I am a survivor. The almighty has never let me down. I am my own role model.

I thank those who have come into my life. All of them have been loving and each of them compassionate in their own way. Whether the interaction was personal or professional, they have taken my interests to heart and acted as they thought worked best for me. They have given me learning experiences by living and working with me. All that I have put down in this book is my own personal perspective and it is up to my readers to take an overall holistic view.

Gratitude

I present here an expression of respect and love to all incredibly beautiful people who have impacted my life significantly. I would like this memoir of mine to be dedicated to them. Together, those I mention have built a safety net for me. They are my love and security system, it's wiser to surrender before the miraculous scope of human generosity and to just keep saying "Thank you", forever and sincerely, for as long as we have voices.

My lifeline, my sunshine, my son: Chikki (Krish)

दवा जब असर न करे तो वो नज़र उतारती है, एक माँ ही होती है जो हार नहीं मानती है: माँ

My support system: Babloo, Neha, Bunty, Hina, Keenya, Samaira, Vihaan

गुरु साक्षात परब्रह्म: Parveen Chaudhary (PC), Abdul Qadar Pasha, Mrs Guptan, Aabha, Anjali Sapra

Heartful gratitude to my mentors for guiding me on the right path: Veena Raizada, Commodore Rakesh

Sardana, Keshav Pathak, Mahesh Dadlani, Swati Anand Kkatyal, Rakesh Verma, Victoria Muir

हर एक दोस्त ज़रूरी होता है: Kavita Yadav, Sunita Sahu, Deepak Singh, Varsha Gunjalkar, Ajay Mishra, Yogesh Sharma, Anoop Gupta

My awesome colleagues: Abhishek Joshi, Sooraj Rana, Swati Arora, Rahul Sharma, Saksham Gosain, Ramandeep Singh, Anuj Kataria, Ujjwal Chakraborty, Sumit Bhowmick, Ankur Sharma, Aviral Maheshwari, Tarun Ojha, Harminder Bhatia, Gaurav Sharma

Valuable professional partners: Piyush Pyasa, Rakesh Sharma, Sachin Vashisht

Informal friendship coach: Shree Shree Amit Dixit jee

Karmic connection: Prabhas

1. Blessed to be ferried in this charismatic world

"I wish that every month of the year was October."
The story began with a bang some forty plus years ago from today, 7th of October 2021. A girl child was born in what was then a small town off Jaipur popularly known as the Pink city of Rajasthan. And she got her nickname, "Pinky", that's me!

I was born into the Marwari community, which is given to many traditional customs, most of them sensible, but not all. There should have been a celebration to welcome the first child of my generation born to the second son of the house. But something was not as it should have been.

"Why was this first born a girl, and not a boy"?

My grandparents had craved for a grandson. But like it or not and much against their expectations, I was there. Perhaps my grandparents would be placated sometime in the future when the grandson they had wished for would be born far away from home, on a distant shore. There would be celebrations in Jaipur when the first grandson did arrive.

As for my parents' generation, the home housed my Dad's two younger sisters, two younger brothers and an elder brother who was known to be a little mentally challenged, but the fact had never been investigated thoroughly.

As for my Mom, this was a small town and the home she would have to live in with her in-laws after she got married. Her first view of this place in the state of Rajasthan had led to her shedding tears. The land was arid and rocky. She was aware that her husband had chosen to live far away on the seashore, in a more hospitable place. He had many duties to attend to at his place of work and would return to his station soon after they were married, whereas, she would have to stay here, with her in-laws.

There were few proper roads or shops for the basic things of life. She did not know if there were institutions of health or education either. What she did know was that here at her in-law's place there were no buses, no busy train terminals and no new-age motorised transport. The main means of transport seemed to be camel-carts, popularly known as *Oonth Gaadi.*

Back in Kanpur, her birth city, this young Mom-to-be had been the apple of her family's eyes as she was the only girl child with four brothers. Compared to this area in the nineteen seventies, her hometown was a large, vibrant city. Maybe I digress, because I would really like to talk about Mom's circumstances before my birth.

When Mom was expecting me, she along with her *bhabhi* (wife of her husband's elder brother) would walk out to a dusty road, hail and board the only means of travel, the camel-cart. They would then travel thirty miles on the rickety contraption, jolted from side to side, so Mom could consult a doctor about her fast-advancing pregnancy.

Still, Mom counted the pros and cons of this existence. A major pro was that her sister-in-law was not only her mainstay, but she was supportive of Mom who was the new addition to the family. She felt it was her duty to accompany and guide a younger soul who was not only pregnant, but also a little lost in this new environment. She was affectionate and would behave like Mom's own elder sister.

Mom bore me, the first child of my generation, and her *bhabhi* extended to her the same esteem and respect not only in words, but in deeds as well. As the first born, I presumed I had a special place in everybody's heart. I was told that my name had been selected based on a well-known "Sanjeev Kumar's" Bollywood movie of that time titled '*Anamika*'.

Mom's *bhabhi* had unfortunately not been able to conceive a child despite being married five years to the elder brother. And here was Mom, who had conceived and was expecting a child within the first year of her marriage! At that time, she was held in high esteem in our family and our society for having achieved this feat.

Mom recounts the story of what happened to me and therefore to her as well. On one occasion, my elder *Chacha,* was near the entrance of our home and My *Daadi*, was on the first floor. On his insistence, she and *Chacha* played a game with me as the object.

The game was that my grandmother should drop me from the first-floor *verandah* and my *Chacha* would catch me downstairs, on the ground-floor. They did this once, and then once more. Though he might have been mentally weak, he prided himself on his quick reflexes and coordination. When *Daadi* dropped me, I believe

I fell accurately into the net of his arms. It was a bulls-eye drop.

I am told that I along with my uncle and grandmother loved it. All three of us were giggling till there was a spoke in this particular wheel of 'fun'. The spoke was my Mom who witnessed the second round of the episode. Her reaction was predictable.

I have heard from Mom that seeing the incident, she felt that she would have a heart attack, and maybe she did have a small episode. But she overcame her feelings on account of her good sense and mothering instincts.

Even today, it is fresh in her memory, and she tells it as though it happened yesterday, she can clearly see the visuals. At the time, she knew she had to decide and put the plan into action. The day of the game with me as centrepiece, was the day she decided that she and her daughter would not stay in that house. She felt that both of us needed a change of scene and better protection for me. At times I feel, I have got my inner strength from my mother. Even today she continues to amaze me with her ideas and immense knowledge.

Dad, in far-away Bombay (Mumbai, as it is called today), had a most respectable job in the Indian Navy. She decided that he would look after us till I was grown enough to take care of myself.

Given the limited means of communication at that time, my Mom wrote a longish letter to my Dad, explaining the specifics about what had happened and how she thought the problem should be solved. To make sure that the letter got to the right person, Mom had to hail a camel cart on that dusty road and head for the nearest post office. Mom's endeavour to get through to Dad was successful.

Dad reacted as was expected. He took up the incident with his family and spoke about the solution. As could be predicted, he agreed to bring both of us to Bombay. As was my grandmother's nature, her parting words were, "I am letting you go to Bombay as you have given birth to a girl. Had it been a boy, I would have made you stay with me in our *gaon*".

For Mom it was a relief. She thanked God for bringing a daughter into her life so that she could live with her husband away from the restricted thinking, risk-taking set-up.

Mom has many memories of me and of that time, which I in my early forties, can clearly visualise because of the way she has told me. I was a premature baby, born within seven and a half months of her pregnancy. Sometimes I wonder if that camel cart ride could have contributed to my premature birth.

My early birth meant that I did not look like other babies. Mom says that if I had not been her own, I could be described as a new-born, shrunken baby monkey with dusky skin and large brown eyes. I was kept in the incubator for fifteen days so that my vital organs could develop, and I could get the right amount of oxygen. The *silsila* of hospital that started with my birth continues till date as I keep landing in hospitals often.

Mom has other memories to relate. She had come to the only cosmopolitan city of India - Mumbai, then known as Bombay, the city of dreams and the financial capital of India. People's mindsets were quite different here. Officers' wives loved this larger setting. I don't suppose my family and I were too concerned at that time about this jewel in India and even in Asia. We were happy for now, having escaped to the facilities afforded by a secure home.

Navy Nagar that we had arrived in, might as well be a small town without the small-town mentality. Dad's job was transferable, so the family would see newer and newer shores, all beautifully laid out. Plus, the accommodation was always adequate to the extent that we loved our homes.

Of course, when I arrived in this city of dreams, I was barely a few weeks old and quite unaware of what had driven Mom and me here, or of Navy Nagar itself. I grew, as did my siblings when they arrived, to depend on Mom's awesome memory about many of our childhood incidents. I can say that Mom revelled in those positive incidents and memories. I can also say that Mom relives our childhood when she tells us the stories of what happened with each or any or all of us.

Dad's interests and job remained in the sphere of a naval officer's duties. He dedicated his life to his work and I spent my earliest childhood in Navy Nagar, Bombay within the security of my parent's love, and the facilities afforded to Dad.

My first conscious awareness is of residing in this pretty place. The house we lived in overlooked the grandeur of "The Arabian Sea". From our vantage upper window, the sea appeared both muddy and blue, depending on the season, for the monsoon could bring thrilling house-high swells, their white-capped tops growing as they crashed onto the shore.

The Arabian Sea, offered Dad the means of his livelihood. Beautiful as it may seem, the navy was always vigilant about enemy ships and submarines and even smugglers on these high seas. I was happy to gaze out at the endless horizon dotted by ships far far away and spin stories in my head about this ocean.

As I grew up, I realised that the cantonment of Navy Nagar had been established some 270 years ago out of an island called the Old Woman's Island, by our colonial peers. Had they known what it would be like nearly 300 years later when they had built that causeway to connect the island to the mainland? Some of the old landmarks such as a church and a lighthouse still exist, while other government institutions have been added.

At home, things were getting more than busy. "Babloo", my cute little baby brother, arrived when I was just a year and a half old. He was born in Ashwini hospital inside Navy Nagar, one of the many facilities afforded to naval personnel. Mom liked the hospitals' name so much that she coined him ... "Ashwini", though at home he was Babloo.

In hospital, Mom had few other worries...what if the babies got switched in the huge ward with just bed numbers for beds and babies, especially when the new-borns were taken to be bathed? Well, we know that Mom came home with her Babloo alright because his looks took to Mom, unlike dark-skinned me who was modelled after Dad's family till I was four years old, when my skin began to lighten. A girl's colour made a difference in my Marwari community, but thankfully, not in our family unit headed by Dad.

I was waiting at home for my live, fair and curly haired, ultra-active naughty new toy. I loved this cute plaything. Mom was worried on how she would take care of two babies as I was still crawling. She says that

I started to walk the very day he was born, much to her surprise.

The other person waiting for Mom and the new baby at home was Dad's sister, my *Bua*. She had assisted Mom during her pregnancy and looked after me while she was in hospital for a week. *Taijee* (Mom's *bhabhi*) would conceive a child after both Babloo and I had been born.

My grandmother would finally celebrate the birth of a grandson in our village. She had distributed *laddoos* in the village for everyone to rejoice at the news of his birth. There is a strange tradition in my community. If a girl child is born, *Barfi* is distributed and if a boy child is born, its *laddoos*. Such gender biasness in sweets too which continues even today. Good gracious!

The rituals among us Marwaris are followed with the birth of a boy. On the sixth night of his birth, there was a gathering for a *pooja* as it is believed that *Vidhaata* quietly enters the house on this day and writes the destiny of the new-born. Mom conducted the pooja smoothly, till the phone rang after midnight. It would be a time of disaster after the joy.

She'd been happy beyond reason at the birth of my brother and such excess joy had led to her passing. The news was that my grandmother in the village had suffered a heart attack and was no more. Sad!!

Dad was grief stricken and the family left for his ancestral home. Mom was my *Daadi's* favourite bahu and had some nice memories of her Mom-in-law, but not too many.

We returned to Bombay after a month since Dad had to resume his naval duties. I have faint memories of being taken by Mom to the Hanging Gardens on Malabar Hill, with both me and Babloo in twinning attires. I remember that he would never walk, but run, fall, pick himself up and run again, despite Mom's vigilance. Babloo was very energetic even then and is so now too.

As my consciousness unfolded, I became aware that Mom was due to have another baby and that she would go home to Dad's village for this baby. Babloo and I tagged along. I picturise this scene of her carrying us as "Mother India". All our relatives exclaimed when they saw me, at how grown I was, and how I was no longer the dark little girl. I had turned into a fair cute baby doll who had started speaking a few words in English. I became a toy for them as they prided in exhibiting me in front of other distant relatives and peers. I would perform in comfortable environment else I would start crying and act stubborn. I can now relate that I had "selective mutism".

The company of little kids in the village was good for me and must have been so for Babloo as well, because by now my *Tai jee* had produced many cousins for us. Gone were the days of her childlessness. Mom could now safely have her third baby without major speculation as to whether it would be a boy or a girl.

Still, everyone was overjoyed when my parents' third child was a boy. This was our Bunty, the youngest in our family, born exactly an year after Babloo. He was named Amit, after "The Amitabh Bachchan", the Bollywood's "Angry Young man", and also keeping in sync with his elder siblings' names which began with the letter 'A'. Ironically, as he grew, he is tagged as an angry young man by all the siblings including our cousins.

2. My formative toddler years

I must have been four or five years old when our family moved out of Navy Nagar in Bombay to Okha, Gujarat on Dad's next posting.

Babloo seemed to enjoy the travel I remember. Dad, as before, was absorbed in the naval work at the massive, busy seaport which belonged to the Indian Navy.

Mom was busy setting up house and taking care of my youngest baby brother Bunty and the house. She saw to it that I start out in the Central School at Okha, which took in children like me without a murmur. These are a network of schools for children of government employees on transferable jobs. As the families relocate, sometimes on short notice, admissions are seamless.

Do I remember that school? Not really. But I do remember an angelic young teacher who seemed to love me and my classmates in that section of the youngest children. I also remember that all I wanted was to hurry home to my siblings. It was so much fun just being with them, as Mom was for most of the day. I would love to have been there all day as well.

As we grew up, I heard her explaining to us on the importance of education. It was she who inculcated in us a love of education, of wanting to be the best at every stage, in school and college and at work.

Anyhow, here we were in Okha, situated on a narrow strip of land that projects into the sea, a promontory. The naval area with residences is also surrounded by sea on three sides and the layout and comforts were not too different from the ones in Navy Nagar in Mumbai.

Mom was happy to have the local Naval officers' wives visit our house, but her focus would always be her family. What struck us was the wide stretch of sandy beach on the Arabian Sea coast. It became a favourite pastime to go down there in the evening and walk along the shoreline, with gentle ripples from the sea washing our feet.

My parents told us about a seaport on the lee side, *Bet Dwarka*, the possible birthplace of Lord *Krishna*, was many miles to the south. *Bet Dwarka* lies on the other side of a small creek from Okha port. On some occasions, Mom would visit the place with us and offer prayers at this holy pilgrimage spot.

Sometimes relatives from Dad's hometown visited us and went for pilgrimage, specially at the *Krishna* temple. They believed that this was one of the *Char Dhams* across India. According to our Hindu scriptures, these are places of worship for those who want to purify their souls. Since my childhood was spent in the birth city of *Krishna*, maybe that is why he is my favourite deity.

There is an episode in Lord *Krishna's* life when his beloved *Radha* asks him annoyingly – "The entire world worships you and everything is just about you?" Krishna being a very devoted lover, responds – "*Hey Radhe*, from today onwards whenever people chant your name, their hurt will reduce to half while their blessings will double". The day I understood the essence of the Supreme, chanting has been a part of my daily ritual and greeting "*Radhe Radhe*". Chanting undoubtedly has divine powers!!

On Dad's next posting from Okha, we crossed Jamnagar and passed Rajkot to Kandla, near Gandhidham city, again in Gujarat. It would have been a short distance across the sea inlet, but we had to take the journey along the Rann of Kutch. We children were fascinated by what looked like a desert of lumpy white sand, but Mom said that these were saltwater marshes that the Rann was famous for.

Dad's postings with the Indian Navy continued and we moved all the way to Cochin. This was where my mind sharpened and began to form images of what I saw in my environment at home, in school and in 'our' larger township in Kochi, home to the Southern Naval Command.

Cochin, or Kochi is a vibrant city, the first port in India marked as a direct entry point from Europe by the Portuguese and later by the British. In my memory, this was the largest city I had seen.

Our family remained close knit and as before, I would still want to go home as soon as the school bell rang at the end of the day.

Mom tells me that I used to gracefully recite poems in school. At home too, she would ask me to recite poems to both my little brothers. I don't know how much Bunty could understand, but Babloo would giggle. I can still feel that laugh. I would sing quite a few lullabies and still remember some of them, with little idea that these would be used later in my life when I would give birth to my son.

It was always fun at home, where I was the leader among the three of us. We recited poetry, played games and told stories to each other as we were growing up. Later, Babloo also joined Central School in Kochi. Dad would drop us to school in the morning before going to work and Mom would pick us up after school. Our home was near the seashore. We would all go for walks in the evening, dig our toes in the sand and feast on ice-creams. I developed a deep love for the beach, the seashore and this remains with me even today. I love the sea more than the mountains. Mom would buy us the *Seengdaana* and *Murmure*, popular snacks of those times in West India, which we would munch on the seashores.

However, Kochi was where Dad began to dwell on matters outside his immediate post and on his family back in the village. He was required to take care of his birth family and their needs more than he had to in the past many years while he had been with the Indian Navy.

Back in Rajasthan, in our village, Dad was seen as holding the most stable job with a regular income. He was the sole earning member of the entire family which was growing by the day and was regularly asked for financial favours which he willingly provided as a disciplined man. He realised that he would have to ensure not only our education, but that of all his nieces and nephews as well.

He liked to see a job through to completion. Dad was the second son of the family but had taken the role of heading the family for his brothers and sisters. It meant that though Babloo, Bunty and I were secure in the framework of Kendriya Vidyalayas, courtesy his job, he was also footing the education bills for all our cousins and he had resolved to do so always.

Kochi was where Dad realised that his pockets could stretch only so far and no further. He had to look for alternative, better paying posts, yet maintain a career in what he did best. It had to be within the Navy, for that was where his experience lay. Dad had garnered many years of worthwhile experience and knew that his job value was greater than what the Indian Navy could afford by way of his pay cheques.

Before he took a step towards a better paying career, we moved once more. Dad was transferred to Jamnagar. It was here that he looked around and sure enough, found that he could be of value in the Merchant Navy. The problem was that he would have to take voluntary retirement from his beloved Indian Navy to join the Merchant Navy, a better paying industry.

Dad's new job also meant that he would have to be on the high seas, away from home for lengths of time. It meant that he had to decide where to relocate and station his family, a place that would best suit his growing children and be good enough for his wife to run the household as she always had. This decision meant that we had to vacate the naval premises and stay in a rented accommodation in Bombay which would be an expensive affair.

After a great deal of mulling over what would suit us best, Dad decided on Gurgaon, a city near Delhi in the state of Haryana. I was hardly ten years old when we moved to Gurgaon.

3. Advancing to a city which had no existence on the map

After spending nearly a decade in coastal towns around the west of India, Dad moved his home base to "Gurgaon".

Situated just on the outskirts of Delhi, Gurgaon was a suburb of the national capital in the eighties and still largely not built upon. Of course, this wasn't the reason for his deciding to relocate. He decided to base the family here for several reasons. He had a cousin sister who had been married to a decorated Major in the Indian army. During the Bangladesh Liberation war of 1971, he passed away in the course of the war and she was awarded with a gas agency as a benefit of being a war widow. The lady was well-known among her peers.

Since he was close to this cousin, he thought we would be safe in the vicinity of his close relative. Back then, Gurgaon was a small town, still to be officially named Gurugram after the *Guru* of two long ago dynasties of the epic *Mahabharata*. Compared to Mumbai or even Cochin, Gùrgaon had little or no infrastructure.

"Even today, I would say that Gurgaon is *be-kaar* without a car".

Compared to the larger urban sprawls we had lived in, this small town had little culture of its own. Mom was worried as she felt that Gurgaon seemed to be ruled by the *Bahubalis* of the surrounding *Jaat* community of Haryana who had lush green acres of land. Though it was unsettling for all of us, it was too late to back out. To me, Mumbai will always remain my first love as I have spent my childhood there. Sadly, we had no choice and were too young to resist or even protest.

During the mid-1980s, Gurgaon started to change. Maruti found a home in Gurgaon and Gurgaon finally found a spot on the map. Thanks to the Central Government which decided to promote private companies as they set out to manufacture passenger cars. That in turn led to the establishment of subsidiary companies and manufacturers resulting in Thousands of Rupees being poured into Gurgaon. Good wages further meant that people began to look for improved standards of living. The city started developing.

There were very limited options of schools to choose from. The school admission process was difficult because in the absence of Kendriya Vidyalayas it had to be a private school. Mom chose Our Lady of Fatima Convent High School, the best in the vicinity. The school was co-educational, with classes up to the tenth grade. As a convent school, Our Lady of Fatima (OLF) was run on strict terms.

The Principal, Sister Precidda was particular about choosing her students. She was known to turn up her nose at most applicants. Luckily, the three of us – both my brothers and me, had arrived from a disciplined school with an organised background and were able to crack the entrance and the interview fairly well.

To me the school was huge. It had grounds for basketball, an assembly ground with a stage for prayer, a playground, and a table tennis room, besides a vast building for all the classrooms with sections for each class.

The school grounds included a lawn with rose flowers around the edges, all tended by *maali kaaka*. He took care and maintained an immaculate lawn. He used to be so engrossed in his work that he did not even notice us all, just the plants, flowers and the grass. Come what may, we have never seen the lawn dirty.

Then, there was a pretty little church. Entry to the church was restricted after prayers before class, which began at 8.00 in the morning. I loved its serene aura. So, I used to go to school a little early to pray. The sister there would give me a pastry as blessing. I must have good food memory, for the taste of that pastry is still fresh in my mind. I can say that I haven't found that taste anywhere else. Even today, whenever I pass by the school premises, my head automatically bows down as a thankful gesture for my learnings from there.

I developed a liking for indoor sports when I joined OLF. I was already into table tennis and made good use of the table tennis room in the school.

I have often declared that my batch had the best teachers in the school. They were the real Gurus. Though I was a mediocre student back then, I was still the apple of the eyes of my Maths and Physics teachers. Till today, Algebra remains one of my favourite subjects. I still love solving equations and maths problems.

Mrs Guptan, the mathematics teacher, was a Keralite. The backbenchers would laugh when she pronounced her 'M' as 'Yem' and 'X' became 'Yex'. The naughty ones used to mimic her accent, and even I allowed myself to giggle as I sat in the front row. I could be naughty too, when a teacher was absent. It meant that I would carefully avoid being seeing by the eyes of the substitute teacher, skip the classroom and go to the playground to play!

All this was in the year 1985 when the former Prime Minister Rajiv Gandhi created an IT revolution and schools adopted an additional subject - Computers. I was fascinated by the computers in school, even though at heart, dance had been my first love. In the end I challenged myself to choose computer classes rather than opting for dance class.

When I did join Computers, it was love at first sight for me. I began to understand the subject logic as taught in the class. There weren't enough machines to go around, so we were made to sit in pairs on each. I was paired with "Kavita Yadav", who went on to become my best friend until we got married and got busy with our lives. I remember her as a straightforward, simple, homely, talented and down-to-earth girl.

In school, the two of us often spent time together after our classes got over. Neither of our parents allowed us to gallivant on our own, but we did spend the day in each other's homes by turn. She too had two younger siblings like me, but a sister and a brother, unlike two brothers as in my case.

I have heard that she has done well as the founder director, psychologist, parenting coach and counselling expert of a company "JiNa - living positively". I'm glad that her positivity has been tapped by way of her work.

As we became senior students, we made many friends. Our gang of friends now included *Bindaas* boys. It was a time of innocence as most of the boys were *Raakhi* brothers. At that time the boys gladly let the girls tie *Raakhis* on their wrists and even gave them gifts in return. "Dipendra Yadav" was one such *Raakhi* brother of mine. He was cute and chubby and extremely caring. We all spent our free time chatting or playing pranks and generally having fun, though studies were also a part of our agenda.

That was school. At the home front, my parents decided that a complete and thorough renovation was needed for our house with separate bedrooms for each of their brood. We moved into rented accommodation which belonged to a Senior Inspector of Police, "Mr Khan". He had a decent family of a wife and six children. We loved the man as he gave us a sense of security and safety. To us he was Khan Uncle, a man who was most respectful towards women.

One of Khan Uncle's three daughters became another very good friend of mine. His family lived on the ground floor, while my family was on the first floor. His bungalow took up all of thousand square yards, with large grounds. My friend and I would spend quality time in this space, walking and talking. A *mawlawi* used to come to teach Urdu to my friend. I also had the urge to learn about the culture and thankfully, he was okay to have me sit with my friend and taught me some important aspects of the Holy Quran. I also learnt the alphabets of Urdu – *'Alif' 'bay' 'pay'*…. Sadly, Khan Uncle passed away in a road accident and the studies stopped. I could only learn the alphabets and no sentence formation. That put an end to my Urdu lessons, though I still love the language and have developed an inclination towards the urdu shayari.

One day, while I was getting ready for school and enjoying my cup of Bournvita on our balcony, I saw two very smart-looking boys zooming around on a remarkable motorbike. It was a Yezdi from Ideal Jawa.

I looked with interest as I recognized one of the boys as my classmate in class IX. I was all of fifteen years old, and so should he have been, I realised. Had he got a motorbike driving license? It appeared that these two boys were the only ones at the time who drove a motorbike to school and back. It was the bicycle or the school bus for the rest of us.

I cycled to school on this day, a happy-go-lucky girl of fifteen, and was myself *bindaas* about most matters. When I reached school that day, the fact clicked in my head that the boy I had seen that very morning wearing the school uniform heading towards school, was missing in class.

I refer to him as "RG". My mind was agog with curiosity, my brain working furiously. I wondered why a student who had started out before I had, and that too on a bike, had still not reached school?

I waited a while to see if he would pop up in class but by half-time, he still had not. A disciplined stickler for rules and regulations, I went into the Staff Room and updated my Class Teacher "Mrs Guptan". She acted on my information and called his parents to school the next day and RG was reprimanded. None of us had realised earlier that we lived near each other. Now, I knew, but RG still did not.

I couldn't have hidden myself for long. One fine day he found out that I lived right across his home. He started following me and would hand out mild threats for being the sneak.

A year passed. We turned sixteen and completed our last year at OLF. Everyone knew that there would be a farewell party as the school was only till X standard. All the girls dressed daintily for the party and looked like fairies while the boys looked dapper. Everyone was excited as we brought along our autograph diaries, asking our batch mates and teachers to sign autograph, and promising to be in touch forever. In those days, we would have these fancy autograph diaries which we used to get from the Archies store. I also bought one for the special occasion and it was passed on to the friends to write parting messages.

The girls counted the number of proposals each had received. I got four, out of which two were expected, one unexpected and the fourth a surprise, as it was from RG. I gave it to RG and he'd written a line in my autograph book which went – "When the sun is shining and the sky is blue, when you are thinking of others, won't you think of me?" Amazingly, I remember the lines till date. The message didn't end there. He also added that he was looking forward for my reaction. Somehow, he got it into his head that my reply was in the affirmative.

This was the beginning of my troubled love story.

The board results were expected to be declared shortly. When they did, we had to go to school for our results. I had butterflies in my stomach and too scared to go. RG, on the other hand, was not only good in studies but he was outstanding and would often get 100/100 in all the scoring subjects. He zoomed off on his bike to Our Lady's for the results. He found out that both of us had passed with good grades and to my surprise I topped the school in Hindi! Hindi? Me? Oh my God! I still chuckle when I think of it. May be the examiner was in a very good mood that day.

He zipped back to my place to tell me and my parents about his and my results. Mom was pleased with this harbinger of good news and treated RG to a tall glass of mango shake. He brought the conversation around to what was uppermost in his mind...what should the next step be? I could see that he was zeroing in on me, wanting to know which school would I enrol in now?

Eventually, RG took admission in Air Force Golden Jubilee School along with his friend and my Rakhi brother Dipendra. He tried but couldn't find out from me where I would go. He was clever and found out from my brothers. I went to Rotary Public School (RPS), as Mom wished. RG withdrew from the Air Force Golden Jubilee and joined RPS.

Rotary Public School was the only school in Gurgaon which was till XII and ensured school board examinations. Else, I would have had to go all the way to Delhi thirty miles each way.

RG asked, and found out which stream I had enrolled myself in. I had taken Physics-Chemistry-Mathematics (PCM) with Computer Science as my additional subject. My best friend Kavita also joined RPS, but with humanities.

It took some adjustment, because compared to the Our Lady of Fatima's sprawling grounds, this was much smaller. So was the school building with high boundary walls. Today, the school has shifted its base and is quite huge. The school seemed like jail with many cells as classrooms. I wonder who the architect was. At times the students felt that once in there, we were cut off from the world. There was hardly any playground, but yes, the best part was that it had a canteen where we could get samosas and a cutting chai.

Unlike OLF which was very strict, RPS was liberal in terms of how students behaved and dressed. Like every other girl of my batch, I persuaded my Mom to shorten the length of my skirt and got my legs waxed. It appeared as though I was getting ready for a fashion show rather than for school. Such innocent were the school days when you focussed only on enjoying every moment. I terribly miss those days of innocence.

Contrary to the school building, the teaching staff was wonderful. There was "Parveen Chaudhary", known by his nick name PC amongst the students and his peer group. He was lean and around six feet tall, with silky hair and a big mole on his cheek. He would be in his early thirties and was a chain smoker. All the girls and boys giggled and decided that PC Sir looked more like a hero rather than a teacher. We created a song which we all sang within ourselves:

"A hand-rolled cigarette to smoke,
Another one bought from the store.
If he lights one, his mind's lit up
Another one burns a hole."

PC Sir, along with our computer teacher "Abdul Qadar Pasha" for C++, and "Pushkarna" Sir who taught Physics to the PCB section, made up a trio. In school, they were known as the Trimurti and were good friends.

PC Sir was our Class Teacher as long as I was in RPS. And I was one of his favourite students and likewise. He was very strict and blunt when it came to submitting assignments and keeping up with studies. At first, PC

Sir's strictness kept me out of school for a week with supposed fever. I was too scared by his looks alone.

The mere idea of going to school gave me high fever. Mom guessed that something was wrong. She spoke to me on the fourth day of my absence from school. I told her that it was my Class Teacher, and it was not that he had ever scolded me, but that it was the way he was - scary!

PC Sir lived nearby. One morning Mom took me to his place. He was respectful to her, and she told him the truth about my absence from school. He was a Jaat and had that "Jaatly" tone. He snubbed, "*Ya toh isko padha lo, yaa phir ghar baitha lo*". Not that he was annoyed, it was just the famous *Jaat* tone. And the sweet and sour relationship that started back then, continues even today. Since that day, he supported me in the best possible way.

But here comes the twist, my rapport with PC Sir wouldn't go down well later with RG.

And few days into the school, came the *"Mandal Commission"*.

7th August 1990, when I was in class XI, "Vishwanath Pratap Singh", the Prime Minister at the time, announced that Other Backward Classes (OBCs) would get twenty seven per cent reservation in jobs in Central Government services and Public Sector units. This would take the total number of reservations for Scheduled Castes and Scheduled Tribes to forty-nine per cent.

The decision of the Mandal commission didn't go well with the masses. Soon after VP Singh's announcement, protests rocked the country. Many students took to the streets, holding dharnas and blocking roads. These evolved into anti-Mandal protests, which took an ugly turn in September 1990 when a Delhi University student from Deshbandhu College, Rajeev Goswami, self-immolated. Goswami became the face of the anti-Mandal movement at that point.

As a result of the protest, we saw the first shutdown of its kind. Colleges, universities and schools were forcefully closed. It was study from home back then for almost three months. Unlike today, where the kids are having online assignments and online classes, we were confused and were forced to have holidays with no advisory from anywhere. Somehow, the school authorities managed to courier us the assignments which none of the students of my batch completed as we were all busy enjoying the unanticipated holidays. We gave the assignments a perfect ignore.

For me, I was in my own thinking zone, I was happy that God had found a solution for me as I no longer had to find excuses to not go to school, as per RG's guidelines.

Eventually, schools reopened after few fake promises by the Congress government. And after we resumed school, young people being what they are, it was broadcasted that I was a favourite of PC sir. The school grapevine created further problems. When RG found out how well PC Sir treated me, he didn't take it very well. He barred me from going to school. I was young and thought this possessiveness as love. I stopped going to school for the second time.

This time PC Sir noticed my absence and started asking around. He must have got a hint as to what was wrong, because he knew for a fact that I was happy in school after I had started getting along with him. So, he knew that there must be some other reason. Since he had a great network, it didn't take him long to guess the reason. He then came home to understand the problem. I told him that I couldn't come to school as I was scared to go against any statement or command laid down by RG.

He advised that he come to my home, provide notes, and teach me Physics. The only allowance being a cup of *chai* with sugar. He seemed to be a tea lover too, just like me. Sometimes, Abdul Qadar Pasha, would also accompany him. I found out that either he or Pushkarna Sir brought PC Sir over because he did not drive. All three of them endeavoured to see that my understanding of their subjects progressed. That was how my senior school studies were managed.

RG had been adamant that I should not go to school. The very thought of me talking with boys alarmed him and worse, was taken out on me in this manner. I went back to school when he relented, under the condition that I do not communicate with boys. It hurt because it included Dipendra, who must have been hurt too, especially when he was barred from visiting my place for *Raakhi* as well.

Not only Dipendra and me could no longer be friends, but my best friend Kavita too could see his unsettling behaviour. She chose to maintain a distance as she didn't like me dating him or may be for some other undisclosed reasons, and the friendship started to dwindle. I waited for RG to mature, to see the sense of things because I thought that I was committed to him by then. I could see that I was getting hemmed in, losing good people and good friends, but I did not rebel or went against him. Now I realise that the worst part was that I never discussed these issues with any of my friends, which I now think I should have. I had to bear the brunt of being called arrogant as I suddenly stopped communicating with them.

It was not only weird but was also getting very difficult. I had support from Mom and PC Sir, not to mention the other two Sirs who had stepped out of their school room box to support and assist me in this direction.

I went through this crucial phase of my life courtesy RG, somehow cleared my boards, credit "THE PARVEEN CHAUDHARY"

4. Summer vacations and beyond school

Mom was the decision maker at home back then and continues to be so even today. Neither Babloo nor Bunty nor I could go against her decisions. Since both my brothers are younger to me, they hardly interfered in my affairs or argued with me. I could always be bossy with them. Our family roles were highly structured and in place.

As for me, I was like a princess straight from Disney world. I always had my own room unlike my brothers who had to share a bedroom. Not only did I have a bedroom with an attached restroom, but a study as well. I had everything that any girl could ask for. The room was adorned with a number of Barbie dolls and my cupboard was filled with the best of dresses with matching shoes.

Since Dad sailed across Europe and America, he would come home laden with gifts which had still not come into the market in India. I bathed in luxurious lather of Camay soap, shampooed my hair with the best of imported ones, wore French perfumes.... you name it and I had it. I did not even think about struggle or poverty, and I hardly knew what career or savings meant.

When we were in school, we not only visited him on his huge ship but even sailed with him during every school summer vacation. We loved what we saw during those trips. There was always a lavish buffet and oh… the special treats! I remember marmalades and imported cans of coke and assorted cereals. And those large swimming pools, Babloo and I would squeal in delight, rush into life jackets over our swimming gear and jump into the sparkling water. Babloo swam like a professional whereas, I would just play around in the pool.

The swimming pool and the water were Bunty's hates. Today Bunty is a champion swimmer, even if he might have been a little scared of Dad and his drive for his children to do better and better back then. We put it down to the fact that Dad expected all his children to be disciplined along the lines of the Indian Navy personnel. Even when my brothers grew up, he would instruct them in good habits. One was to shave daily and keep a *Fauji* haircut. They did as they pleased most of the time but would follow Dad's strictures when he was home.

Mom was an expert chauffer of the Ambassador car that we had. She would drive me anywhere I wanted to go and even pick me up. Being the only girl child, my Mom and my brothers were very protective towards me.

I loved it. I admit that I was an extremely pampered child who could get everything without asking. Style and beauty came naturally to me. I was told that I had beauty, brains, attitude, and money stamped on my persona, a complete package.

It might have been a coincidence, but all three of us took to science with the PCM combination in our high school. While I was moving to class XII, Babloo got admission in Mount Carmel School in Delhi. He was an all-rounder, marvellous at sports and studies. He would always be rated among the best in class, and he always got top scores.

I had cleared my boards and wondered what I should do next. I was in love, though the relationship with my boyfriend had not gone all that well. The famous phrase of actor Kareena Kapoor fitted so well with me then – *"Bachpan se hi mujhe shaadi karne ka bada shauk tha"* I was naïve enough to think that all relationships were similar to mine and would progress towards one end.... marriage. I had one and only one dream – to get married to this love of my life and settle down with him. I did not plan or have space in my mind for a career.

The only person in my family who had thought about a career for me was Mom. She had dreamt of me being a doctor or an engineer like every parent of that time. Since I had a non-medical combination of subjects in school, she settled on Computer Science Engineering as my next study option and career. During the mid-ninety's, admission into an engineering college was difficult and there were hardly any colleges in North India. Most of them were in the South or the West. Adept as she was at finding out and taking charge, she zeroed in on to Bharati Vidyapeeth College of Engineering in Pune.

Dad was away sailing right then. Mom took the help of one of his cousins, boarded the flight to Pune with him and managed to grab a seat for me in Computer Science Engineering. When she came back, she organised a small get together to celebrate this success. Her daughter would join one of the best engineering colleges in Pune.

Were my relatives truly happy? She soon found out that there had been gossip behind her back. One of them even said to her face — "It's just the admission, you are celebrating as if she is already an engineer". Mom kept her peace. These were the same relatives that Dad doted on. They were the reason he'd resigned from the Indian Navy and moved the family to Gurgaon!

As for me, I was lost in my own dreams. I knew that Mom knew best and that I would study Computer Science at Bharati Vidyapeeth College of Engineering, Pune and live away from home. But I had other more important (to me) thoughts on my mind. For example… Which college was RG taking admission in? When would I see him? How would we be together in a world that was bent on keeping us apart?

RG and I thought that these were impositions. Why, we were adults, and could run away and marry? After all, we were eighteen years old! But the people we confided in, those we thought were helping us to marry, gave away our secret. Our parents got to know, and it was embarrassing. On hindsight, I can say that it was just as well.

It was even more embarrassing when we were made to promise not to get in touch with each other till we completed engineering college. I went off to Bharati Vidyapeeth Engineering College in Pune, and he was sent to Shimoga, a small town near Bangalore, to pursue Mechanical Engineering.

Even in the '90s, Shimoga was known as a higher education centre in Karnataka. There, RG had been enrolled in Jawaharlal Nehru National College of Engineering. However, neither of us knew where the other had gone to study. There were no means of communication, especially after that promise we had made to our parents.

Finally, it was time for me to leave home and travel to Pune. Pampered as I was, and as the family presumed, I flew down with two of them in tow...Mom and Babloo.

I arrived at the Bharati Vidyapeeth College campus in Pune and decided to familiarise myself with the surroundings. I had already found out that this campus was premium among all the Pune colleges. It was spread across 85 acres of land and known as the Katraj Campus, with 24 college disciplines, mainly a Medical College, Dental College, and the College of Engineering, where I would be.

My college was on the Satara Road, which was on the outskirts of Pune at that time. The campus extended beyond educational facilities to the Bharati Hospital and an Ayurveda and Homeopathic Hospital. There were hostels for both girls and boys with no-go zones in between, and canteens with mess facility. The grounds were well-maintained, and our surroundings were green.

Before Mom left, she introduced me to one of Dad's colleague's son, "Deepak Singh". He was over six feet tall and very good looking. He was a third-year Mechanical Engineering student. Our parents had known each other since their Mumbai days and Deepak had grown up speaking fluent Marathi.

When I met him, I found that he was relaxed and easy to get to know, besides being someone who understood where my family and I came from. He was staying in a rented apartment in the vicinity of the campus along with another student "Samir Seth" who was a Gujju in the final year of Computer Science Engineering.

Deepak was "Deepak Bhaiya" to me, and we became close friends, practically siblings, and our respect for each other was mutual. Deepak was popular and macho. He drove a bike and lived by his own rules, smoking and occasionally having a drink.

When I first set eyes on my girls' hostel room, it was a shock. It was nowhere near what I was used to at home. I was expected to share the room with two other girls and queue up outside a common bathroom with my own bucket and mug and soap and shampoo etc etc every morning! Ultimately, I found a time when there were few girls in the washroom. It meant that I could shower and bathe at my own pace without someone banging on the door asking me to hurry up. I guess this last was the fate of latecomers!

When I first saw the hostel facilities I was like – "Shit, is this what is called a hostel?" Mom and my brother had not left. I threw tantrums and persuaded Mom to take me back. I had never stayed away from Mom, not even for a single day. She somehow made me understand and stay on. Then, my family left, and I was alone. This was the first time and I missed her and my brothers sorely.

The girls in the hostel did not have too many rules. They would laugh, talk loudly and keep the lights on into the wee hours of the night, whereas I was a quiet shy girl who had adopted the rule of "early to bed and early to rise makes you healthy, wealthy and wise". I slept early and woke up early. Besides, in my princessy bedroom at home, I slept with the lights off. Now, I had to get used to three beds in a L-shaped room. I took the bed at the furthest corner of the L, hoping to get as far away as possible from the other two beds and their lights. But that was not to be. The other girls would not sleep till half past midnight.

I pretended by keeping my eyelids shut tight, faking sleep in my bed. In truth, I was shedding tears behind those eyelids, hardly breathing, thinking about what this night in my own home with my family around me would be like. I was agonising away from them, missing home life and the security and privacy of my room and my bed.

Ragging was a common "norm" in those days for freshers and it was a perturbing. I had heard about ragging and was terrified at the mere thought of extent the seniors could go. And me being me, can get stubborn in front of strangers when it comes to performing. My room mates were equally scared and somehow, we got the information that it would happen at the fresher's party.

On the eve of the fresher's party, I developed fever and was successful in skipping. I was very happy about my achievement. It didn't last long though. Seniors always kept the track of who didn't get ragged. One day, some seniors stopped me on my way back from classes and started passing absurd comments. Deepak and Samir passed by on Deepak's bike with a "*sutta*" in one hand and "*katta*" hidden in his jeans pocket. Filmy, no? Deepak realised what was going on, stopped his bike and said loudly, "Anamika, go to your hostel". Such was the intensity of that sentence that even today, the thought of the scene gives me goosebumps.

The air around us was electric. I left. The boys who were trying to harass me came up in the mess next day during breakfast. Our hostels had strict boundaries, but the mess was common, albeit with separate entry and exit points for girls and boys. So, this group of boys met me and apologised for their behaviour. That was the beginning of a strong bond between Deepak, Samir and me.

Samir had a friend who was in the same hostel as me. She was also in Computer Science Engineering like me, but in the final year. "Varsha Gunjalkar" was also reputed to have top notch Bollywood connections through her brother Prashant Gunjalkar, popularly known as Ganesh in the film industry and a producer by profession. He simultaneously ran a few other businesses and is a closest friend of "Salman Khan", the popular 'bad boy' of Bollywood and also the object of my childhood crush.

Deepak, Samir, Varsha and I formed a well-known friendly foursome on the campus.

Deepak taught me how to ride the motorbike. Samir had a Kinetic, so Varsha learnt to ride that. Deepak could do a piercing whistle and taught me how to whistle the most amazing *seeti* in his own style. I am proud to say that I haven't met any girl who can beat me at it. I might have been able to out-whistle boys as well. I am happy and simultaneously proud to report that my inner child is still ageless.

Deepak, Samir and Varsha...all three of them were my seniors. I was a fresher and much junior to them. They set themselves up as my guardians. I can also say that I was pampered by them and felt safe in their company. We would have breakfast together at a *Tapri*, a shanty tea stall, strategically situated at the corner of a street in particular.

Tapris tended to mushroom outside any college campus, near offices and outside railway stations. They served small breakfast snack, *Vada Pav*, my favourite local fast-food dish. It is native to Maharashtra, and I had learnt to love it years ago as a child. The deep-fried dumpling in a bread bun came with one or more *chutneys* and green chili pepper. Inexpensive street food in Mumbai, the *Vada Pav* has acquired connoisseur status for refined tastes in restaurants across India. Another nickname is Bombay Burger on account of its looks and origin.

Maharashtrians and Mumbaikars of today have claimed the delectable snack as being part of their food culture. I remember taking numerous flights to meet Varsha and Deepak to eat *Vada Pav*. Back in college, I preferred it anytime from 'our' *Tapri*. We used to eat there because the food was not up to my taste in the hostel mess. I discovered that *Tapri* thanks to my friends. Having found it, I would linger, filling myself with tasty *Vada Pavs*. Because of the *Tapri* I did not starve or take the flight back to Gurgaon, desperate for normal vegetarian food.

Honestly, I would have been crying for Mom to not send me back if I hadn't met these three musketeers. What I ate on the campus was *Poha* with Bournvita in the morning, *Khichri* in my both meals, afternoon and at night. The cooks would serve bitter gourd in the gravy giving me the feel of a crocodile swimming in water. The *Bhindis* aka okra and the other *sabzees* were cooked in coconut oil with lots of garlic. This, when I just could not stand the smell of garlic!

While on this topic, I had also thought that I would not date anyone who was a non-vegetarian or who ate garlic. It's not that I hate non-vegetarians or have anything against them, it's just a personal preference. But then, life is never simple nor was it ever meant to be. RG was a hard core non vegetarian and a garlic eater.

The four of us close friends would plan outings over weekends. We explored places like Mahabaleshwar and Lonavala on Deepak's bike and Samir's Kinetic. In my memory, I can see all of us at that time and truthfully say that those were the best days of my life. My friends filled my soul and a large portion of my heart, though RG remained firmly in there.

Deepak is now Vice President with TW Ship Management, Mumbai. Varsha took voluntary exit after heading Revenue Assurance at Reliance Communications for more than two decades. Varsha's love interest and later husband Vinayak worked at Reliance too, and today heads the engineering function at the Reliance refinery in Jamnagar. He is an amazing personality for whom I have much respect, one of the nicest and loving persons I have ever met amogst husbands of my friends.

Vinayak remains a loving family man whose other main interest is his work. From what I have seen and heard, Varsha will always adore the way he is, while his colleagues always speak highly of him.

Pune plays a prominent part in my story. One day Varsha and I borrowed a Kinetic from one of her friends and went for a ride. I was riding. Deepak and Samir were busy elsewhere, so we girls decided to go shopping at the Benetton store on MG Road. We bought a couple of tops for ourselves, ate sumptuous delicacies at Aurora Towers and started back. We were on top of the world in respect of new clothes, excellent lunch and each other's company.

We thought we had the world at our feet, and we were happy enough to sing a popular Hindi movie song - "*zindgi ek safar hai suhana, yahan kal kya ho, kisne jaana*", at the top of our lungs as we zipped along.

And suddenly, we skidded ....and.......
I blacked out.

I was obviously too confident for my own good and quite unprepared when from nowhere a cow appeared, wanting to cross the road. I braked and tried to swerve to save her. But the Kinetic had been zipping at high speed and when I braked, it skidded.

When I regained my senses, I was in Bhagali Hospital on Satara Road. My right leg was elephantine. I was bruised everywhere. Thankfully Varsha was fine and had a few bruises. She was standing beside me holding my hand. An X-ray showed that my right knee was badly crushed, and I needed surgery for which the hospital required my parents' signature.

As Dad was away at his job, Mom flew to Pune the very next day and a surgical team was called from Mumbai. Though the meniscus knee tear surgery went off successfully, but wires had to be inserted in my right knee joint which I got removed recently by having another major operation. Varsha and Deepak visited daily while I was in hospital and did everything in their capacity to make me feel comfortable. They spoke about the incident and got on well with Mom.

The Doctor notified, what had happened to me was significantly crucial, that I would be able to walk after five to six months, even then it might not be normal. He recommended crutches for support for the next six months. He even mentioned that I would never be able to walk straight and would limp forever. Mom was devastated beyond words after hearing but kept her calm and never showed her fear. I spent some four weeks in hospital, flew back to Delhi and then got driven to Gurgaon. I couldn't move from my bed for over a month. I did begin to walk as the doctor had said, but with crutches and that too baby steps of only five to seven steps at one go.

I was thankful that my knee surgery had been conducted in Pune because compared to that city, the medical facilities in Gurgaon were not all that great. Now, the herculean task was to find a physiotherapist. With great difficulty and loaded with references, we could arrange one and he agreed to train a few exercises which I had to do daily on my own for half an hour. And me being me, I hated exercise and had been living a sedentary lifestyle forever, but the situation demanded, and I managed somehow.

RG's Mom came to know of my accident and planned to have a visit at my place. When Mom got to know, she hid my crutches in the storeroom and instructed me and my brothers not to mention a single word around it. Why was Mom worried? Perhaps she did not want my current condition to ruin the prospect of marriage. A mother's anxieties remain, whether they are affected by traditional roles in society or not.

5. Road to recovery and beyond

I stayed at home for nearly six months to recuperate. It affected my study and I could not attend my second semester of my engineering course.

That meant that I would have to repeat my first year to continue in computer sciences at Bharati Vidyapeeth, whereas my batch mates had been promoted on to second year. I hated the idea of going back to scratch. I had never had to repeat any class or any subject. It was a jolt. I could not bear the idea of studying with my juniors while my peer group would become a year senior.

My Mom and my brothers tried to prevail on me that going back and starting again was the best option, but I was adamant. I could not bring myself to explain to them that I had lost confidence and how bad I was feeling. I blamed myself. There was also the fact that Mom had thrown a big party when I got that admission to engineering college, and here I was refusing to go back. Even today, after thirty years of the incident, on special occasions my relatives broach this subject just to demean me and my self-esteem that I am a dropout of engineering.

I adore a statement from one of my friend, "Gaurav Sharma", who says, "*parivaarwaad equates to atankwaad"*. And it fits perfectly in this situation and a couple more as the story moves forward. Some of the relatives never shy away from making you feel bad about you and yourself. Pity though!

I never went back to Bharati Vidyapeeth.

I didn't even go back to collect my belongings. The relationship with Deepak, Varsha and Samir, all my friendships were put on hold. I remember Yatin Tewari, Mridul Chaudhary, Kinjal, Suvina Jain and the daughter of the famous villain Roopesh Kumar of the historical Hindi movie *'Seeta aur Geeta'* in my first-year batch. Mumtaj Khan Farashahi, the movie villain's daughter was a pretty girl. She too left in the first semester.

Unfortunately, I am not in touch with any of those friends of mine, except Varsha and Deepak. I know that Samir settled in Canada. I could not bring myself to communicate with anyone outside Gurgaon.

Not only did this incident drain my confidence, but I started having sleepless nights. What was going around in my head was the broken leg, the broken study line and therefore, would-be career and separately, a broken heart. Nothing seemed to be going right. I had bouts of anxiety and depression. During this phase I became very close to my brothers. They heard me and gave me their full support.

Babloo scored excellently in his boards and was preparing to join the Merchant Navy, like Dad. He was so brilliant in studies that had he decided to opt for civil services, he would have easily cracked it. But he adulated Dad and wanted to follow in his footsteps. Mom supported him in his decision, though Dad also thought that Babloo's brilliance should lead to greater things. As usual Mom won. After many discussions Dad gave in. He went ahead and joined as a naval cadet.

My brother's career was set and here I was at home, thinking about how and what to do with my life. It was not that I had not liked the stream that Mom had chosen for me.... Computer Science, but ...to repeat a year! No ways!!

Eventually, it took me almost a year to recuperate from my surgery. It was the most difficult phase of my life as I went over and over the same facts, without being able to crystallise my thoughts.

I landed into the world of confusion.

To find some peace and solution, I took to reading whatever I could get hold of. I used to regularly read the "Ascent" section in the newspaper. Times Ascent, a part of The Times of India, is focused on career enhancement, jobs, upskill courses, latest events, and trending news etc. One day I saw an advertisement for a short-term course in programming from NIIT. I discussed it with Mom, and she agreed to finance. It was a two-year software course and by the time I completed it, I would be job-ready before my earlier batchmates in Pune. I enrolled for the course.

At NIIT I liked what I was learning and doing. But not before I remembered how RG would say that he didn't approve of higher education for women and that he wanted an undergrad partner for himself! So, when he knew I had dropped engineering, he was happy to pop back into my life.

When he came to meet me at my place, it was to find that I had joined NIIT.

He rushed to the NIIT centre and indulged in a frightful dramatic scene, demanding that the centre manager let me out from the ongoing class. The administration there were scared of this kind of behaviour and so was I.

What was I thinking? That this was how a man truly in love behaved? At NIIT I realised that I had been forced to surrender and came back home with RG. But I could be strong too and worked out things to suit me!

When RG came home on vacations from Jawaharlal Nehru National College of Engineering in Shimoga, I stayed away from NIIT. I was able to successfully cover up the fact that I was continuing there. It was only when he went back to Shimoga, that I attended the classes. I suppose it was my way of self-preservation, my own manner of doing what I had to do, while I tried to show him that I had given in to doing what he wanted me to.

Once I joined NIIT and had gone back to an organised life with the security provided at home, my confidence began to return. I made friends again and was totally drawn to what I was learning. I began to enjoy my life and did not doubt myself, even as I made room for how to deal with RG's demands.

"Sunita" became a close friend. I met her at NIIT, and she went on to become my soul sister. She was beautiful, tall, and had a curvy figure and she was a couple of years older to me, like my close friends at Bharati Vidyapeeth in Pune. Age however is just a number, and we gelled well and got along with each other. She was from a middle-class family, and they were two brothers and two sisters.

Sunita's family had also had a brush with tragedy after her sister's husband died in a car accident within three years after her sister had given birth to two girls. Going forward, her elder brother would marry only after Sunita got married, but at that time she was too young for marriage.

After classes, Sunita and I liked to chat in a garden near the centre. We talked about our futures over tea and *samosas* from the shack at the gates. The man who ran this *Tapri* got to know us and would wave to indicate that he knew what we would order. Soon enough, he would come running with our tea and *samosas*, and we would happily chat, drink tea and munch the eats.

As for what we chatted about, we had this dream of setting up an NGO for disabled children. Both Sunita and I had sheltered upbringings, felt for the downtrodden, and unaware that we would have to first stand on our own feet with support from everyone possible. We did not think that we would first have to take care of our own daily needs before we thought of anyone else.

I also met "Anjali", who was my teacher at NIIT. She was a good-looking Maharashtrian girl from Mumbai. She'd married a Punjabi of her own choice and moved to Gurgaon. She was only slightly older than Sunita and me. I could say that all three of us - Sunita, Anjali and I were fairly close in age, with me being the youngest and therefore, the most protected by the other two.

Anjali reminded me of Varsha, my other Maharashtrian old college friend. I missed Varsha and compared her with Anjali. I realised that Anjali's personality was very different, even as she filled the void in my heart left by Varsha's absence. In her own way, Anjali was brilliant and energetic about what she did.

Sunita did not seem to be too fond of RG. She did not approve of my relationship and maybe, could see what I could not. As a down-to-earth person, Sunita

< 44 >

has lived the difficult times of my life with me. I was always drawn to people who are very down-to-earth and practical, without showing off their social status or bank balance.

RG's visits from college were becoming frequent. There was no Internet, no phones during those times, hence we could only spend time together when he was on vacation from his college. The communication was less and coming from a conservative family, meeting boys was a strict 'no' from my Mom. But I knew by that time that she liked RG very much and appreciated his personality and hence, allowed him to visit home sometimes.

RG would visit my home frequently and would stay for hours. I tried to make him understand that this isn't the right approach, but he would not listen. The relatives and society started murmuring but no excuse would stop him from creating nuisance. Hence, one day my Mom approached his parents for a match between the two of us and suggested a ring ceremony so that the *gupshup* could be stopped.

Mom was trying to quell any unnecessary murmurs in the community, she told me. But my future Mom-in-law, or my MIL-to-be, put down a very straight forward condition. She said that any engagement between her son and me would have to wait till her elder son's wedding. The discussions did not go smoothly. RG belonged to a family of three boys and a sister who was the youngest and the most sensible amongst her siblings. RG was the second son. His sister treated me with respect and was loving. She is married in a respectable family and is now settled in Canada. I don't remember any incident wherein she ever troubled me.

My Mom wasn't very happy with the condition, and she again tried to explain and suggested a solution to RG's Mom, "At least these two can get engaged and in the meantime, you can look for a bride for your eldest". In the entire incident and conversation, she got annoyed at RG as she sensed his lack of support in this venture and his commitment towards me.

RG was busy getting unreasonable without cause on occasions, lashing out by physically tormenting me. It even happened when there were known people around watching him. Ironically, this happened in front of my near and dear ones and his friends and family but strangely, no one condemned him for his behaviour. What was tough for me was not being able to talk to anyone, because I think no one understood what I was going through. I knew what I was feeling but I couldn't communicate as I was under pressure to be a very "supportive girlfriend".

Some comments and complaints must have reached his parents', but they turned a deaf ear and a blind eye towards such incidents. I found out later that such culture was common at their place. But what about me and my opinion? Today I have nothing to say for myself but at that time I knew that I wanted matters to normalize, I wanted to marry and start a family in the way that girls of my age did.

Mom had managed to keep the channels open for discussion with RG's family about when could we have the ring ceremony and when could she announce our engagement? One fine day after a great deal of discussions between the two Moms, the date of the ring ceremony was finalized.

The situation was so aggravated that Mom had to decide about the ceremony while Dad was away as the only solution. She had wanted a date after RG's family said 'yes'. Mom must have also noticed that RG was getting more demanding with each passing day, and she did not want to take any chances. It was to be a very small get together with close members of both families.

The day when RGs family arrived, his parents were missing. They had asked his grandmother, his Dad's sister and brother-in-law, and RG's siblings along with two of his best friends to attend the engagement ceremony. Mom presumed that the old lady was representing his parents. It did not seem right at all if neither his Dad nor his Mom were going to be a part of the first function of their family.

From my side, Mom was very much there since Dad was sailing. Then there was Dad's cousin sister, the Army Major's widow, and my Dad's elder brother's wife who had been an important person in Mom's life. Being her closest sister-in-law, Mom valued her enough to hardly ever organise any function or even a small pooja without consulting her. My aunt's elder daughter and son-in-law and both her sons came too. In my family I have seen the affection the *bahus* have for each other, be it on my paternal or maternal side. They have always exemplified the respect and love for one another.

Like many other Moms, she hoped and thought that things would settle down after we had a stamp on our relationship. She had arranged a photographer, a videographer, catering, and everything required in such a function. RG arrived in casual wear.... jeans with a white shirt and a sleeveless black jacket over it. Whereas, I had taken the opportunity to dress up and was in a white and golden organza lehenga with a skin-coloured brocade top to match. I had chosen gold dangler earrings, been to the hairdresser to blow dry my shoulder length hair and left them loose with a side parting.

If I was perfect for my own ring ceremony, so were Mom's arrangements. She had decorated our place with flowers and lights as the occasion required. Mom had also put in her best cooked vegetarian dishes known to our community and was pleased when the fare on the table was appreciated by our guests.

My brothers were very much a part of my formal ring ceremony and were dressed appropriately for a function like this. My side of the family were fully decked up, but RG's parents were not only absent, but we realised that his family did not even think of this as a special occasion.

They came in casuals, as had RG. We were slightly disappointed but chose to ignore and said nothing. Mom was happy that this day was being celebrated, as can be seen in the photographs clicked on that day. I am her only daughter and the first child of our family, she loved me since the day I was born and had travelled across the country for our sakes even when I was the tiniest baby.

Mom welcomed each member with a gold *ginni*. The celebrations and festive spirits were genuine, and we finally exchanged rings. Joy and politeness in place, the boy's side left after the function, till RG called later that evening to say that they had been kicked out of the house by his Dad.

Reason?? He complained that he had not been informed about the engagement!!

Phew, what was this?

My Mom had been discussing this ring ceremony with his mother for almost a year now! And this reaction? We were all stunned. All the happiness turned to gloom in no time.

RG's father, after throwing the family out of his home, was living alone while the rest of the family got themselves a rented apartment just three houses away. This was indeed a family who had lived through much drama! In fact, I am still unclear on why he thought he had not been told about the engagement and why the others were all thrown out of the house to move three houses away in the same neighbourhood. It was the strangest turn of events and baffled me completely.

Most people would have been worried about neighbourhood gossip. I found out later that their neighbours were used to the goings-on in this family and that the family also did not care about them. It followed that RG's parents hardly bothered about what he did, or maybe they ignored it when he did whatever he wanted to do.

As always, I blamed myself for this act too, and at nights kept thinking about a solution sulking alone by the pillow side. One day, I mustered enough courage to go and see his Dad. He was still keyed up and lectured me. After a long time during which I got to speak as well, I got him to agree to call back his family to live under his roof. And that was such a relief! I had been having sleepless nights and the day RGs family went back, I could grab a little sleep.

After that memorable engagement, I remember an outing to watch the movie 'Border' along with RG'S elder brother, his sister and one of his friends. We went to the movie hall Priya which was one of the most happening theatres in Delhi at that time. It came to a scene where India's second-in-command in the army played by the Bollywood actor "Akshaye Khanna", was dying. It was an intensely emotional scene, and I could not help sobbing.

I heard, then felt a smack, something which took a few seconds to register.

RG had slapped me hard in the theatre and was shouting, saying, "Why are you crying, I am alive. He is not your husband"!

There was pin drop silence as the rest of us sat there, rooted to the spot and shocked.

I felt humiliated, hurt, and shamed. At the time I also felt that he was right, and I was wrong, that I should not have cried, it was just a movie. I told myself that this was RG's way of saying that he could not bear to see tears in my eyes. I told myself that this was because he loved me. I'm older now and know better that it was his male chauvinism. But I still wanted to marry him, thinking that "may be" after marriage things will settle down.

At that time, I was young and had very little sense that "may be" doesn't work and I should have taken a note of my sixth sense. But I was madly in love and as they say, "love is blind", unlike today's Gen Z who have redefined the quote as "Love may be blind but not us".

Prima facie, my in-laws seemed to like me and were loving towards me, but they would turn a blind eye and a deaf ear when I tried to talk with them about matters of importance concerning RG. Sometimes it was urgent and important, but I would be rebuffed because they thought I had come up with a silly complaint about his behaviour.

Time flew by. Another three years passed since our engagement, but there were no signs of the wedding date being fixed. My future mother-in-law was sticking to the rule she had set down - her elder son to get married before her second son could marry. In the meantime, Mom was getting impatient as my courtship period was getting prolonged.

Every time Mom sent a message to his family pressing for finalization of the marriage date there would be a blunt reply. "Unless and until I get my elder son married, RG will not marry". Mom would get stressed and did not want to accept this answer. She finally got them to agree to a wedding date. But again, there was drama, though less than the last time.

It came to a point when there were hardly six days left for my wedding, as per the invitation cards sent out. It was the next day, that is five days before my wedding, that we were informed that they had found a bride for the eldest. His elder brother to get married in the morning, and we were to marry later in the evening the same day.

6. Kalyanam aka Lagna

My wedding date had been decided by our family *Panditjee*, February 1st, in the year 1998. It was also *Vasant Panchami* the spring festival and was also celebrated as *Saraswati Pooja*. The *tithi* is considered to be an auspicious day for any wedding. Our *Panditjee* had also mentioned other good wedding dates, but those were later in the year, and this was the one that my parents selected. They had thought it over and decided that after a three year long engagement, an early wedding would be the best.

My family had several discussions amongst themselves and with RG's family regarding the wedding and the rituals related to it. There was no end-result but a lot of confusion which I will relate as my story unfolds. My parents and immediate family were determined to do the best for the wedding of their eldest child and much-loved daughter.

Bunty had completed his graduation and was preparing for his entrance to management studies. Babloo was also busy in his career. He liked what he was doing but missed the family. I guess that is the hardest part of being in the Merchant Navy. It was difficult, as he could not make it to my wedding. I felt terrible that my brother would not be there to witness this milestone in my life. During my ring ceremony, my Dad had not been there, and now Babloo! As a sister I was sad, but neither of us could do anything about it.

The fact was that neither RG's family, nor my extended family were too happy about a marriage outside our respective communities.

Babloo was away sailing, and my *bua* and her family refused to come to an inter-community wedding. *Bua* did not even call, her decision hurt. More so because I was her favourite niece and I gelled very well with her. My maternal uncle was also not there to take part in the pooja, probably for the same reasons as my close relatives on Dad's side.

I was downcast!!

In my childhood, he too had declared that I was his favourite niece, as had my *bua*. All in all, there were many niggling problems and absences from both my paternal and maternal sides. All the rituals which were supposedly to be done by my maternal uncle were undertaken by my *Taai jee's* younger brother, "*Pappu Mama*", as I lovingly addressed him. I have a deep respect for him.

I was determined to make the most of my wedding day in the way I looked, in the traditions of my *Rajasthani Marwari* community and advice of the elders. I would have gladly been a Sabyasachi bride. However, his wedding outfit creations were not around at the time. The designer started his business later. I chose to design the wedding dress myself. We went to South Extension, Delhi to buy the material. I decided to go against the traditional red colour and wore a golden brocade lehenga-choli with intricate gold work.

Was I going to be the radiant bride? I was thinking loud in my head.

I also sported the traditional *Rajasthani maang tikka* known as *Borla*. What else? Oh yes...the green bangles which are adorned by brides from my state, a symbol of auspiciousness and fertility, worn only by brides-to-be or married women. I stuck to all the dressing rules of my community because I wanted to.

Since my wedding was the first in my generation, it was a very grand affair. My parents arranged a lavish 'do' at a resort, the "Wet n Wild Resort" some miles away from Gurgaon.

I got into the SUV waiting to take me there with Bunty, Pappu *mama* and "Deepu", my favourite cousin sister with much anticipation. The driver skilfully navigated over unmarked speed breakers in the rain, because of hardly any streetlights making use of the SUV's headlights. The driver went over one such speed breaker, when we realised that we were slightly airborne, and the SUV was out of control. Would he ram the truck ahead? No, but there was a thud as the vehicle landed back onto the road.

In addition to my disquiet at the many absences, I wonder if that was a heaven-sent sign towards what was to come, not that I had any such thoughts then. We thanked God for saving our lives. Bunty took control behind the wheel as the driver was not comfortable after the incident and his legs were shaking.

Finally, we reached the Wet 'n' Wild Resort, took note of the lavish arrangements that Dad had asked for and then headed for a room dedicated for me till I would emerge at the appointed hour of the wedding (we had been brought up to be punctual). My family hoped that since I had come on time and the venue was as we wished, matters would go smoothly henceforth.

My bridal ensemble and jewellery were in place as I had envisioned. We had arrived by half past eight, in good time for the *muhurat* at nine at night. My friends Anjali, Kavita and Sunita, visited one-by-one into the bridal suite where I was lodged. Anjali arrived with her better half, unlike the others who were happily single. After wishing me luck as I start life's new journey, she left for the main venue. I was told that the guests had also started arriving. Kavita and Sunita stayed with me and all of us waited for the groom's side to arrive.

Everyone waited....and waited.... and waited.....

RG and his family were aware of the *muhurat* time, and we hoped they would arrive by nine. We made excuses to ourselves on their behalf for their prolongation. It could be because his elder brother had married that very morning. They had even taken the green metallic coloured Zen which Dad had gifted me. The brand-new car had arrived six days ahead of the wedding.

But, as true for any Punjabi family, the *Baraat* took their own sweet time and the wedding rituals started only at midnight after an adequate amount of time had been spent in merriment. The pre-wedding drinks were practically a ritual with them. Many of them including RG, were in a heavily drunken state.

If my vegetarian, no alcohol-drinking-at-home, tradition-following and mild-mannered family was shocked, they tried not to reveal. However, this excessively late, drunken arrival was something else altogether.

The time of the *Jaimaala* where the bride and groom exchange garlands had passed by and most of our guests had already left. Still, it was a wedding and there was a *Jaimaala*, even as I sensed murmurs about a drunk groom.

RG was accompanied by a local *Jaat* friend. We set about trying to exchange garlands on the stage which had been arranged for this purpose (though the groom was not steady on his feet). As I was about to put the garland around his neck, his friend pushed him away and I missed.

This may have been part of the teasing that went with a wedding, but after a few attempts I stood up and told RG and his grinning friend that I would not try again, unless he stood still. His younger brother rescued the situation. He removed that friend of RG's from the stage. The ceremony finally got going and continued through.

I think of his brother today and picture the incident, unfortunately, he passed away during the pandemic. May God bless his kind soul in everlasting peace! He was a beautiful soul, a great human being and very loving towards me.

The *Mandap* in Hindu weddings is the central decorated element, the 'sanctum sanctorum' where the actual wedding rituals are conducted. A select number of people need to be present, main being the bride, the groom, their immediate families, and the officiating priests. It was now time for the *Pheras*.

I paid complete attention to the beauty of my wedding and was aware that in Hindu religion even the smallest gesture has cultural or religious significance. The Holy fire was lit with wood, *ghee* and other *samigree* in the *Havan Kund* following which we took the seven vows. According to Hindu mythology, fire is one of the five natural elements (*Panch Tatva)* that make up the human body. It signifies the eternal bond between the couple even as fire separates them from each other.

The seating arrangement during the seven vows had also been carefully planned. I was initially seated on the right-hand side of the groom; but after the completion of the vows, I was placed on RG's left, indicating that I was now closer to his heart. This was ironic, as my story will show.

In the seventh and last vow, he declared "we are now husband and wife, and we will stay together for eternity." This was as per custom, while I replied that with God as our witness, I was now his legally wedded wife. I understand the institution of marriage differently now. The word legal has spoiled it. You legally wed and legally separate. Quite satirical!!

The final ritual is the *Vidaai*, the ceremony organized by the bride's family to officially bid farewell to the daughter as she leaves for her marital home. Being RG, he had instructed me beforehand to not show any signs of emotion at this point. He did not want me to be crying during this 'going away' ceremony. He'd threatened to punch me right there if I did. I tried hard but couldn't stop myself from weeping at the thought of leaving my loving and caring birth family. Even today, when I watch the videos and photographs of my wedding, I get goose bumps.

I was leaving, and moved towards Dad's lavish gift of a car, the metallic green Maruti Zen, parked close by. Sadly, the morning's flower decorations for RG's brother's wedding had wilted. The brand-new car was not at its best and in a bad state by the time of my farewell. It even smelled of stale booze and non-vegetarian food. There were used disposable glasses inside. It was disappointing, particularly when we had taken so much care, giving attention to every small detail at the Wet 'n Wild Resort.

The portents for a happy married life were not so good.

I shook myself off such thoughts, got into the car and sped off on the long drive to RG's home. Enroute, I dreamt of a beautiful life. I reached his home and entered as a bride should.

Another shock awaited me there! The moment I entered my supposed bedroom, all my dreams regarding my special night were shattered. Not only was the mattress bare, without a bedcover, but the gifts from my parents were piled higgledy-piggledy on top of the bed. Imagine, an air conditioner and a television set lying on the bed of the newly wed. Other brand-new gifts were scattered haphazardly all over the floor. I had tears in my eyes, but I didn't allow them to roll down.

I was stunned to see the room and drew myself up to ask RG about this.... "had no one considered that the bed should have been made, considering this was our room"? My heart cried at seeing my welcome into the family.

RG was drunk and this query did not suit him. He got into a rage, more than the offhand reactions I had earlier seen. He threw the TV from its precarious position on the bed. The TV screen shattered, as was expected.

I was mortified at such a scene with so many relatives in this new home of mine.

Was this to be my welcome?

7. Sibling Bonds

*R*aksha Bandhan, September 2021. My thoughts wander as I continue to miss my brothers and their families on days such as this. It extends to every evening when I spend time on my balcony, visualising the days of our happy childhood and the close bonds we have forged going into adulthood.

On this day of "*Raakhi*", sisters, whether younger or older, tie a thread around the wrists of their brothers. It is a popular Hindu festival celebrated in my part of the world. The thread is sacred, a symbol of protection for the sister, woman of his family or a friend close enough to be considered a sister. The brother offers a gift in return for his sister's kindness and thoughtfulness.

Raksha Bandhan is observed on the last day of the Hindu lunar calendar month of *Shraavana*, which typically falls in August every year. Babloo was away, sailing. He has achieved maximum seniority as Captain of his ship, sailing the world somewhere around South America. I couriered the *Rakhi* to him since he was not going to be at home in Gurgaon. He had hardly been home during festivals. I miss him badly on such occasions and so does he.

Bunty and his family were back from London and were stationed in Bengaluru. I had planned to fly down to tie the *Rakhi* in person on Bunty's wrist, besides wanting to meet "Hina" (his wife) and "Keenya", their 9-year-old son. What intervened and put an end to my plans was the tail end of the second wave of COVID, while the third wave is still expected.

I cancelled my plans in favour of health security and shared blessings with him, Hina and Keenya by video conference as the new normal of Pandemic times.

Bunty was a shy, middling student till he cleared his XII board examinations. During his school days, he used to often get fever. Babloo and I would go to his friends' place, take down notes and help him to complete his class work and homework. His personality did not open up till much later. In fact, we were all meek and mild children, a little scared about what our strict Dad would say.

I remember one incident when a friend of Dad's visited us. He arrived on a scooter. Like every other boy, Bunty wanted a ride. He was so keen that he confidently told us that he could drive a scooter. Dad's friend handed over the keys to him, but we were careful to ask Bunty to show us just once how he rode it before he drove out onto the road.

We had a big garage and Bunty began to show us his skills. He started the ignition, changed the gear and pressed the accelerator. In the blink of an eye, we saw him and the scooter crash into the still latched main gate. We rushed to pick him up. The scooter was a wreck, but Bunty was not hurt. It was God's grace that he had not ridden out on the road.

We could see that Dad's friend was anguished when he saw his scooter though he said nothing. Mom gave him the money to repair his vehicle which he was very reluctant to take. Today Bunty drives well, but we often laughingly refer to the day he had crashed! It was scary then, but today we remember it heartily and make jokes about it.

Bunty scored excellently in the XII board examination, getting over ninety percent marks. It led to admission into one of the most prestigious colleges in Delhi University in the Commerce field. In college he brushed up even further and came out with flying colours.

By the time he was twenty, Bunty had an all-round personality. He was good at what he did and knew the lay of the land - where to eat, where to shop and a great sense of direction in Delhi. Later, he lived in many cities and honed his radar sense even more. Today we have Google maps, but in those days, he was the equivalent of a Google assistant!!

I have often got stuck in Delhi. When that happened, I would call him to understand which direction I should take. Bunty explained easily, even giving me the exact number of intersections with traffic lights that I should count on my way.

As a child Bunty would throw tantrums when he thought Mom loved *Bhaiya* (Babloo) and *Didi* (me) more. With Babloo it was, "you love *Didi* and Bunty, not me as much"! And I would claim something else, telling Mom that, "you love them more because they are boys". Poor Mom, she was always like, "I love you all and there is nothing more or less love for you three!"

Bunty had his own college affairs and fights which only Babloo and I knew about, because he confided in us.

We would keep each other's secrets. Bunty lived through and survived these easily because Babloo's and mine were always in the limelight, held up for the family to notice. I say mine because of RG's drama, and Babloo because he was fighting to join the Merchant Navy.

While Mom was struggling to resolve our issues, Bunty was calmly going about his life without our Mom ever having to know or even worry about anything. Bunty's social life and ambitions were not broadcast. They hardly ever surfaced. He remained the son who was not any trouble for her and was known to be very caring and loving.

After he graduated, Bunty went straight for a master's in Business Administration. I wryly thought of the time when Babloo and I would do his homework and help to get subject notes for him.

Better still, today he is with Tata Consultancy as an Associate Vice President and doesn't wish to leave TCS, a subsidiary of the Tata Group, the company he has been a part of over last two decades. He often boasts that TCS has the best retention policies in the industry and is confident of his career in his organization until he came to know about my present organization's policies. He has a changed opinion now.

The multinational Tata Consultancy Services are headquartered in Mumbai, though the largest campus is in Chennai, Tamil Nadu and in Bengaluru, where Bunty is. As of February 2021, TCS was seen as the largest IT services company worldwide with market capitalisation of $169.2 billion. Bunty is settled in Edinburgh, capital of Scotland and travels occasionally though by a different mode to Babloo in the Merchant Navy, who travels constantly.

Bunty got married to Hina, a girl with excellent family credentials. She is as mild mannered and modest as her husband. They are probably this way because they are so confident in themselves and with each other; they make a perfect pair. I lovingly call their son Keenya, my distorted version of Kinu.

The boy attended Norbury School in London where they previously stayed before moving to Edinburgh. As a result, his diction and British English are perfect. Kinu is very sweet, polite and the orange (not apple) of everyone's eyes. Orange, because his name is derived from that fruit. He has a knack for video games and can do anything in the world to play them.

Unlike Bunty, who excelled later in studies, Kinu is already a young scholar. He lovingly calls me *Bui*.

I don't remember any incident when all three of us siblings did not come to a consensus. We thought alike and agreed on everything, we were that close.

My brother Babloo and his beautiful wife "Neha" were blessed with twin babies, albeit after they had been married for some seven odd years. Mom took the initiative to travel with Bunty and Hina to seek blessings for all of us from the *Siddhi Vinayak* temple in Mumbai and her prayers were answered. Neha conceived and gave birth to twins "Vihan" and "Samaira".

I remember a very interesting incident from Babloo's wedding. The time on his wedding invitation card was mentioned as eight pm. Mom being the wife of a naval officer was very particular about timings and she always reached the venue well ahead of the time mentioned. We knew from our past experiences that weddings don't start by eight in Punjabi community or for that matter in any community.

Despite all our efforts of getting late, she forced us to get ready and with her disciplined and commanding nature, led us to the venue by eight. As expected, there was not even a single member from the bride side to welcome the *Baraat* and the resort people were still decorating. All three of us siblings got the chance to joke about Mom's planning and acting over smart. How could we let go of the chance of a lifetime to comment on her as we probably would never get such an opportunity ever again.

Finally, after quite a hustle and bustle, a call was made to the bride's parents, and they informed us that it will take them almost an hour to reach.

An hour????? Phew!!

It was decided that we will enter the venue and have some munchies. After being at the venue for an hour or so, we received a call telling us that the bride and her family are fifteen minutes away. The Baraat was asked to assemble back outside. We then started dancing and acted as if we had just come, as if, it was all normal. That was such a hilarious incident and we all still laugh joking about Mom's OCD for timings.

8. What works and what does not

American track and field athlete and four-time Olympic gold medallist Jesse Owens had famously said: "We all have dreams. But to make dreams turn into reality, it takes an awful lot of determination, dedication, self-discipline and effort."

We humans crave for information about the future, as our primary reward. Our brains perceive ambiguity as a threat, as we proceed to create certainty.

I have developed my own philosophy in life based on my own, and the understanding I had from others' life experiences. I know that a good plan can always fall flat if fate has other plans in store for us. In my case, I put myself in the hands of God while taking steps to do better. During the lockdown, I enrolled myself in many courses including "Leadership and Change Management" from IIM.

The Indian Institute of Management is the most prestigious institute in India, ranked at number one. Undertaking an IIM course meant that I could take it up without having to go anywhere and also be able to rest my poor leg. It meant that my forced resting time over weekends could be utilised in activities which I considered a 'must' by now - meditation and up-skilling myself, as I did with the leadership course.

For me, it was a day of quantifying my success when I received the certificate. By now, I am a bachelor's in economics, master's in literature and another master's degree in human resource management. Being proud of my IIM certificates and degrees, I want to ask those relatives, if they would value these over my engineering? But I will not!! I no longer seek people's validation.

I have gone from being a shy, stupid, innocent girl to being badass. The lockdown during the pandemic was when I started to get to know myself. I had ample time to reflect, become self-aware and finally love myself. I shed guilt as to whether I had been wrong in my life and discovered that nobody in the world will come to my rescue. I had to rescue myself, by myself.

I had made mistakes, the biggest of them being that I always looked for validation from my friends, family, and colleagues. In turn, I constantly questioned my own worth, feeling that I had not done the right thing. While writing this book, I came very close to myself and realised the deep meaning and significance of the quote "Love your own self before you love someone else".

I have recently also undergone some sessions with "Harsh Johari", a Leadership Coach. In a couple of those sessions, we discussed my strengths and weaknesses and their aftereffects. It held up a mirror to my inner self, one that I could act upon.

The exercise revealed that my major strength is in the ability to move on. Next, is that I am able to make up my mind about people and don't waver when something goes wrong (yes, that can be a strong point). On the other hand, I don't stint in giving my hundred per cent when I am in a relationship or in a friendship, but once I am warned, I am done. There is no looking back. I make this statement directly from my heart with the many years of experience I have had in life.

Today how people perceive me is the outcome and summation of my life's severe experiences. My coach, "Harsh Johari" asked me one question – "What do you think is the impact or effect of being such a strong personality?" The side effect of being strong is that people don't think twice before hurting you, as they feel that you don't get hurt. They get comfortable as they consider that you will be okay with every damn thing. No, we are not. Even strong people have hearts of the same size as normal people and they do get hurt too.

Today I can tell myself that when I love, I love hard and when I am done, I am done. This is a trait of a strong Libran, as I believe myself to be. I am selectively social and do not open easily to everyone.

He then threw another question at me, "Don't you miss the old friendships and friends? Is this not hurting you? Is it going fine?" I could answer him with confidence because I felt it had worked for me this far. "Yes, I am fine with my broken relationships and friendships", I replied. "Though I haven't forgotten any person I have met, but that doesn't mean I hate them or miss them or regret not being in touch with them. In my opinion, people who have stabbed once will do so again".

When I think about it, all those people that I miss and those that I don't miss, are both important because they have played a significant and definite role in my life. They have taught me the basic lessons of living. These lessons are indefinable, they cannot be studied in school or college as the course curriculum doesn't touch upon the reality. These can only be learnt via "PEOPLE".

I am thankful to each one of them and don't regret even for a second that I met them, because they did have a role to play in my onward journey of life. Today, I am at that stage where I don't argue. When anyone tries too hard to convince me I just say "okay" and put myself on mute. In other words, I do not make my argument known, because I have realised that ultimately it is up to me whether I agree with them or not.

I am now at a point in my life where I have seen and done a lot. It means that I have my own exclusive points of view and respect others in what they have to say even if I do not agree with them. As long as no one imposes their control, their opinion on me, I do not intrude.

Earlier, it was different. I have been a wife and a daughter-in-law, but right now I can look back and reflect at the intervening twenty-four years. Not to mention the fact that I have been formally separated with RG for some twenty-one years of those twenty-four.

When he was my husband, it was a tumultuous time. He had never been a loving partner to me. All I faced was mental and physical abuse in my relationship with him, be it pre, post or peri.

I can think of one incident of that stormy time during my married life. My close friend Sunita whom I had first met at NIIT here in Gurgaon, was to get married just two months after me. Her elder brother came over with the wedding invitation and a box of sweets. I hadn't met her after my marriage as I had been barred from meeting all my friends. I pictured a Jaat wedding, with all its dancing and merriment. I was really looking forward to her wedding and more so, to see and meet her.

I also wanted to show off my newly married self with my husband. After a great deal of persuasion, RG agreed to take me to the wedding. On the day of the wedding, I completed all the household chores allotted to me in good time. I did not want to leave any housework to do at night after we returned. I had been putting up with RG's moods and did not want to give him a chance to point out any flaw. I was worried that he might cancel our very special outing if he found anything to pick on.

I was getting ready in the evening and wore a nice silk saree with matching jewellery. I had long silky black hair in those days, and since I was going for a celebration and wanted to look as good as I could, I left my hair loose. I had very little idea that he would use this as an excuse to not go.

As he entered the room, I asked him if I was looking good enough. I was not ready for what happened next. His face darkened and I heard him yell at the top of his voice. "How dare you leave your hair open! Is it your wedding? Are you going to honeymoon with her groom? You aren't worth taking anywhere. Learn how to behave and dress like a wife"!

With that, RG stalked off, got into the car and drove off at top speed. I stood there zapped. My mind couldn't grasp anything. I didn't have a clue as to what just happened. I was aware that RG's strictures towards me included not being allowed to wear sleeveless or deep necked clothes, but not that I should not be allowed to leave my hair open.

I had thought that trying to look my best, while following the rules of looking like a respectable, decent, recently married woman would be alright. Was it my mistake? My confidence had gone. I was not sure. I missed a dear friend's wedding and wept all night.

9. Great blessing of my life from the Almighty

RG's elder brother who had got married the same day as us, is a father to a beautiful daughter and one son. The baby girl "Ankita" was born exactly a year after they were married. She was the first baby in RG's family and was very dear to her grandmother, Ankita's mother used to accompany *Bhaiya* in his business who was the wholesale dealer in pharmaceutical business. My MIL used to take care of the baby when they were away at work.

I have briefly been *Chachi* to the baby girl, but not the boy who followed, though he must be sixteen years old by now. RG did not like the idea of children and took safety measures accordingly. Since the elder *bahu* of the family had a baby within a year of her marriage, the pressure was turned on me to have one as well.

I would often be asked about this, "When are you going to be a mother?" Some even started suggesting remedies and options. I understood then what my *Taijee* must have gone through since she had conceived after many years of marriage. But in my case, the reason was different - RG had set down the rule.

Happily, 'mistakes' happen!!

When I did conceive an year and a half into my marriage, it was by accident. I remember that when I first realised this, I was on cloud nine and so were my Mom and my brothers. I also know that there was a little fear lurking at the back of my head, would 'they' share my happiness? I was right. There was hardly any joy at my in-laws' though the reasons for which remained unknown.

When I broke the news to RG, the first thing he said was, "I want a boy as we already have a girl in the family. Anku is there". This was not good, since all I hoped was to give birth to a healthy baby, not that I begrudged Anku's arrival. RG might have known that our baby's gender was not in my hands, nor was it important to someone like me.

Both of us had studied science (and done well in Biology at our school boards). We were aware of the X and Y chromosomes and how each parent contributed to the pair, and that women always carried the X, and the baby's sex depended on whether the Dad had sent forth an X or a Y sperm. If the sex chromosomes paired as XY, the cell will grow into a boy baby; else a baby girl would be born and carry XX chromosomes.

I could understand when his parents kept saying the same thing - that they wanted a boy child, but then they did not know the science of what lay behind a baby's sex. I could not will it, no matter how much pressure my husband or in-laws exerted on me.

The nine months I spent at his place were difficult and horrible. It had a physical effect on me besides the discomforts that a pregnancy brings. I contracted asthma and my blood pressure remained on the higher side. I became very pale and had sleepless nights, wondering and worrying about the baby and myself. Knowing RG, I started to get nightmares, what if he throws me out of his home or even kill me for giving birth to a girl child.

I began to regret my decision of marrying him.

I felt the absurd food cravings of pregnancy but did not give in to them at my marital home because I was already scared of the many rules and regulations that I had to face in RG's house. I began to make excuses and used to lie to meet Mom and she would make all the things that I wanted to eat.

RG was not in a job but spent most of his time at his brother's dealership business. There were no earnings between him and me, and he could not even give me money to see the doctor or for any personal stuff. Even after nearly two years of marriage, I was dependent on my birth family for most of the things. Mom bore all my hospital expenses and my daily needs. My confidence as to how I would manage was hitting rock bottom.

I could not ask anyone in his family to support or bear my expenses. I felt awfully isolated. I had gone from being a cherished member of my family, one who could interact with my parents and brothers at any level, to feeling alienated and alone. Was I akin to being a maid at my in-laws, one who took care of all household matters?

I could see that this family lived by few values. I don't have any complaints about my MIL or RG's elder brother except one , "why did they never step in, talk to him or stop him from beating me, from hitting out whenever the mood got to him"? I felt that I had moved from a secure, protected environment to one where I was alone in the midst of many. I tried to defend myself as best as I could. I was determined not to give in to the worst. I had told myself that happy mothers have happy babies.

The 9th of April, 2000 was the most meaningful day of my life. It was the day I gave birth to "Chikki", and he was exactly the baby I had dreamt of. I had him by C-section, but the happiness and joy overpowered the pain of undergoing surgery. I had tears in my eyes when I held him in my arms, I felt blessed.

The day when Chikki was born completely changed my mindset towards mothers. Earlier, I felt I had just been existing. Giving birth gave another meaning to my life. The joy that I felt that day was at a level apart from any other I had experienced so far in my life, and it is what I feel every day as I see him growing up.

As they say, a child's smile is the heart of heaven. There's nothing purer than an innocent child's smile. It was so radiant that every time he smiled at me, I would feel a tug on my heart strings.

Chikki was a healthy baby of seven pounds, so my food cravings and my Mom's care must have helped! I might have been semi-conscious after the surgery, but I clearly heard his first cry.

When I regained consciousness and saw myself back in the room with my Mom holding him, I could have wept, I was that happy. Such perfect tiny hands, a crop of black hair on his head, and the baby swaddled in what looked like soft fur. Mom handed him over to me, and I saw a glimpse of heaven. It was a divine experience and cannot be explained in words. It has to be lived.

Dad and Babloo were away sailing, but Bunty was with me in the hospital. I heard that RG was also present there, but I couldn't sense him nearby. I was discharged from the hospital a week later when my stitches from the Caesarean section began to heal. RG drove us back home. Was he happy, now that he had become a Dad of the boy, he thought he had "ordered"? Would it lead to him being better with me? I was hopeful.

But that did not happen. Our relationship deteriorated day by day. By now my parents could sense what was happening. They began to realise what kind of person RG was, without the earlier charm and generosity he had worked on my family and me. I did not have to spell it out for them. As she had when I came away from the engineering degree course in Pune, Mom did her best to make me understand her point of view. She thought that I should make more of an effort, even if it was to continue in the physically abusive environment.

I guess that was how girls were brought up in Mom's generation. Society expected women and girls to be silent sufferers and my parents were no exception. I don't think parents of any girl approve of her decision to give up on a failed marriage, to leave her husband and to seek divorce.

By the time Chikki was born, I knew that my marriage would not survive for too long. I also realised that I needed to start working so that my son could have a future. How was I to do that without a formal degree?

The man who came to my rescue at this point of time was Abdul Qadar Pasha, my computer teacher in class XI and XII, the subject I claimed to be mine when I had started out in school and then in engineering college.

Based on my course credentials from NIIT, he arranged a job for me as a Trained Graduate Teacher in one of the prestigious schools of those times in Gurgaon. I started teaching classes VIII to X, with the added task of being lab in-charge for Classes XI and XII for students who would come to learn C++ language.

RG was dead against my working in any capacity. It probably hurt his male ego; he shrank at the idea of not being the breadwinner of his family. His dictum was, "females shouldn't go out and work, they belong to kitchen and do the household chores".

In truth, I had also never thought in terms of a career, except to know that I was good at Computer Sciences. But the circumstances had changed, and I needed to do something so that when a crunch came, Chikki and I would not be left high and dry.

After a great many difficult conversations and umpteen rounds of discussions, I managed to convince RG. He set down conditions – one, since the dress code for teachers was a saree, I should wear a blouse with quarter sleeves and covered neckline. Not an inch of skin should show below the nape of my neck or throat.

Secondly, he did not want my Mom to babysit our son when I was teaching. However, when we asked my MIL, she made it clear that she would not be able to look after Chikki in addition to her granddaughter Anku. RG realised that there was no option but to leave Chikki with my Mom while I was away during the day.

There was a third condition. I was supposed to stay away from Pasha Sir and all the male staff of the school. Now this was impossible as he was the one who had offered me the job, and I would have to work closely with him. As I had done before when I undertook my course at NIIT, I kept quiet, yet made a promise that I would keep minimum contact with Abdul Qadar

Pasha. No one in my friend circle, family or even Pasha Sir or PC Sir ever knew why I behaved with an air of arrogance that I had acquired. Nor did I ever mention the reason to anyone.

RG was crafty. He would often show up at the school reception desk to check on me. He would ask if I was there in school or try to snatch a chance to see me talking to someone, no doubt with the intention of creating a scene and insisting that I should leave my job.

Maybe, Pasha Sir or PC Sir remembered their missing student in senior school - me, and the lengths to which they had gone to help me to stay in touch with my lessons. They had come home to teach, making sure that I would be able to sit my board examinations and pass them honourably.

I know I was pushing myself when simultaneously I got admission in a degree course in Economics from Delhi University. Life was more than tough but my degree would ultimately be fruitful. After an early morning start, I came home from school at around 2.00 in the afternoon, rested for about 15 minutes, then saw to it that Chikki had been fed.

The rest of the afternoon would be spent in household chores and taking care of Chikki. I would study at night in the hall when everyone else had gone to sleep. My sister-in-law, RG's sister, was undergoing MBA from Amity University, so I had company as she would also study at that time. We gelled very well, and I wouldn't be exaggerating when I say that if I graduated it was because of her. She would make me study with her, made notes for me and then took mock tests to check that I had got it right.

These were steps I was building one at a time, to make sure that I would be qualified adequately and that I gain enough work experience to be able to stand on my own feet when the time came.

I kept my faith.

10. Curtains down

The final nail in the coffin was when one day RG brutally beat me up after having too many drinks. After which he stormed off leaving my son and me crying alone in the room. As usual, no one from his family entered to ask about us, to show some concern, to ask if we were alright. No one even bothered, there was not a drop of care.

Even today, so many years later, I still can't understand why that was so, why they could not extend a bit of kindness in our hour of distress. Their silence, after I moved to my parents, remains a mystery. I was welcomed at my place when I came with Chikki, but when I told them that I was not going back, it was not received very well.

Mom visited RG's parents many times, but they did not reciprocate similarly. My parents were obviously greatly distressed and disturbed. Perhaps Mom and Dad asked themselves the same queries I had about my in-laws — what did they feel about the situation?

There was no answer.

I knew I had made the right decision. I was determined to file for my freedom and to start a new chapter. Asking for a divorce from RG was not easy. Even on the last day of the final hearing, my Mom visited a temple, praying for the divorce to not happen. I believe the all-seeing God knows and hears all. He was kind and heard my prayers instead of hers. Eventually, Mom accepted my deep unhappiness and the inevitable.

It was finally over. I left my marital home behind. It left a bad taste in all our lives, mingled with a bit of relief in mine. In the end, it was doubly difficult for my parents when they decided to stand by me and Chikki, come what may.

I had not requested any alimony or child support and neither did any of them come forward to want to bear the expenses for their grandchild. Most importantly, no one asked for his custody. And that hit me hard. Ironically, they had wanted a grandson, but they did not want to support Chikki in any way or even ask about his needs. Chikki would be fed, educated, protected and his health needs seen to without any contribution from his father or his father's family.

Again, God was kind. Chikki went through the usual childhood illnesses, through school and college and is today an upright young man minus his father's nature.

I remember the time at RG's when I had very few choices. I might as well have been bonded labour, with no freedom to even wear clothes of my choice. This, despite my clothes sense not being outrageous. I could not partake food of my choice, meet with my family when I wished or attend functions of my closest friends.

Then what had I been about? What had I been trying to prove to anyone, even to myself, when he was always looking to pick on something? Today I wonder why I forced myself to be like that. Was that me at all? Had

I even been myself since I was sixteen, when I first met him and thought that I must fit in with his dictates?

I feel sorry for that me, for being cut off and not knowing what the world was like. My life had revolved around RG and his conditions. When I made a bid for some independence when I was teaching, my concentration would suddenly veer off. I would be wondering whether he'd come to the school that morning to check if I was there? What would ensue if he saw me talking with anyone? I had been scared and intimidated. Had I thought I could live my life in this manner? I imagined RG's eyes watching as I stayed aloof, withdrawn and not participating in any events at school.

When Chikki and I separated from him, it was not easy. There was the question of my self-doubts, "had I done the right thing"? My self-confidence plummeted. I wondered if my extended family, society and friends all saw me as a woman who had no belief in the institution of marriage, and I was looked upon as someone in the wrong. The few women who had separated from their partners and spouses at that time were not looked upon as respectable in the society.

It was the year 2004. I had been living at my parents' and decided to take a break from work. I found the going tough and was not able to concentrate when I needed to. I would cry when I was alone in my room, hardly sleep at night and go up to the terrace to gaze at the stars and the moon.

I spoke with these celestial lights in the absence of anyone else to speak with, to tell them how I was feeling. I felt cut off from the world, that I had no friends. Were the walls closing in on me? Was the world coming to an end?

At home, Bunty was busy with his internship post his MBA and had to focus on his work in order to stabilize his future. Dad had taken voluntary retirement from the Merchant Navy. As a workaholic, he could not just stay home and do nothing. He took up a job in the corporate office of his company in Delhi.

Dad had been sailing for most of his life and worked on ships. He'd not had to drive on roads, but did not want a driver. He began to learn to drive at the Maruti School of Learning. He bought himself a car and took to the road to get to office and back home. It was a long trip...some sixty miles every day, but he liked to stay busy.

Mom as usual kept herself engrossed in maintaining the house chores. She grabbed the responsibility of Chikki and loved him close to her heart, even more than her own children. She says it with conviction now, I love him more than you all three!!

Chikki was turning four and it was time for him to start play school. The thought of leaving my child, my lifeline in somebody else's hands was killing me. I wasn't ready and I felt that neither was he. But I couldn't very well keep him at home always. School, even play school, was for his betterment. I found a play school near our house.

Chikki was so charming that he won the hearts of his teachers. I was very possessive about him and could not trust anyone, barring my Mom and my brothers. I would drop him at school, park my car outside and wait for three hours till his play group was done. It may have been absurd on my part, but I did not have the heart to leave him in somebody else's custody for such a length of time.

I was haunted by thoughts of sudden attacks, as RG would do to me. I was scared of someone hurting my child in my absence. I remained in the car, just to stay nearby. The school staff also knew that I was outside. They would call me when they felt he needed me, and I would pick him up right away. My behaviour probably made no sense to anyone but me.

I was dimly aware that I was struggling with depression. Not only did I feel alone but was lonely as well. I would often get bouts of anxiety, enough to argue with those around me. I felt that nobody liked me. I realised that I had a problem and decided to see someone about it. Consequently, I went to a doctor who prescribed medicines for depression and for insomnia.

The medication was specifically meant to treat anxiety disorder. The doctor mentioned that it would help to decrease abnormal and excessive activity of the nerve cells and calm the brain. But like all such drugs, there were side effects, none of them pleasant.

I was fatigued and my coordination became impaired. I was lost in my own world, creating fantasies through the day. However, I couldn't stop the medication either, as that could cause other problems. In the long run, I could tell it helped me to not only manage but even reduce many of the painful memories of my married life. I was so distressed and traumatized that eventually I got diagnosed with type 2 diabetes. My doctor mentioned it to be a consequence of my stressful life.

Meanwhile, my family was carrying on with their lives. Babloo was eying to being a captain and hence he was working towards his goal. Everyone was busy with their lives barring me. I was still questioning myself and the Almighty, trying to figure out the reason for my existence on this earth. I told myself I would have to do something, maybe study, anything to be able to focus.

By now I had graduated in Economics from Delhi University and had filled forms for the master's course in Literature. I found peace in studies. Books were becoming my best friends. I also read for pleasure and would pick up Femina and Gladrags, the women's magazines. Our newspaper delivery boy would bring publications of my choice along with the newspaper. The magazines had articles about women who had impacted society despite facing obstacles in their life. They were real women who had succeeded, and these articles about real women gave me hope and inspiration.

It was *Dussehra* of 2004. I remember very clearly that it was a Sunday, and all my family members were sitting on the roof, enjoying the festival. The Dussehra ground was hardly 200 metres away from home, and we watched *Ravana* and his two brothers burn to cinders in the great big bonfire set-up for the occasion.

Taijee visited every year on *Dusshera* to watch the celebrations with us. This time her son had also come along as he had plans to sit for an exam in Delhi the next day. Babloo also had to catch an early morning flight to Kolkata for his naval course. Dad was to go off to a workshop for Indian Naval ex-service men organized by his company on the very day the boys had to leave.

Both Mom and Dad were coordinating and working out on who to drop where and how to get to his own workshop.

Dad's big heart had never let him take it easy as he gave all of himself to doing what had to be done for his family and friends. On this occasion, Mom drove Babloo to the airport. Dad drove himself and his nephew to their separate destinations. He warmed at the idea of his meeting, for there would be a celebration meal and drinks.

It was all very well, but the question of whether safety would be ensured or not bothered Mom. She knew that Dad loved his drinks. The National Highway-8 was dangerous, especially with trucks and buses which plied at night, when he intended to return. Mom offloaded her worries on to Dad, and as usual, he assured her of his safety when he left.

That night, around nine we received a call from the station in charge of the *"chowki"* to inform that my father's car had been hit by another vehicle. He mentioned that Dad had been bruised and was being bandaged, that we should pick him up.

Upon hearing the news, Mom of course panicked. She immediately called Dad's family friend and took Bunty, who'd just returned home from work. Chikki had slept by then and when I heard about the "accident", I started pacing up and down on the terrace hoping that everything would be fine. Couple of hours later, when there was still no word, I called Bunty to gauge the situation. He too, repeated what the Inspector had said. "Nothing to worry, we are enroute home". I took a deep breath and waited for them.

They reached home past midnight. I opened the gate and all three of them, Mom, Bunty and the uncle who had gone with them, stepped out of the car.

'Where is Dad"? I questioned and peered inside but could not see him. I had not noticed that Mom had covered her face with the veil and was sobbing quietly. My entire focus had been on looking for Dad.

Finally, I looked up and asked Bunty, "why is Mom crying", "Where is Dad?"

He replied, "Let's get inside home".

I could feel my anxiety rising as I raised my tone, "tell me, where is he? Is he in hospital"?

That's when Bunty looked directly at me, his expression tortured. "Dad is no more", he spoke softly with watery eyes.

I was stunned. I heard Bunty, but it made no sense. I asked him to repeat himself. This could not be true!

Except that it was true. Dad had passed away!!

He had been involved in a deadly road accident. His car was crushed under a trailer when he had been at the wheel and alone in the car. According to the police, the steering wheel had hit his chest hard enough to wound him and lead to internal haemorrhage. The car and the body were in police custody. We would get it early next morning, after the post-mortem had been carried out.

Did we know what had hit us?

Our loss, our despair was inconsolable. I saw darkness around me. I called Babloo immediately. He'd reached Kolkata, but I had to tell him. I spoke four words, *"Babloo, wapas aa ja"*. Babloo did not question me as I had queried Bunty.

Had someone else called him before I had, I would wonder later? He replied, *"Aa raha hoon, Didi"*. I shudder to think about that day, and we rarely talk about it. I have never asked him how he knew that something so major had gone wrong.

Dad's body arrived in the wee hours the next day. Hundreds of people had gathered that morning for his last rites. Mom was weeping inconsolably by now. Her husband had been snatched in an unnatural death.

We didn't know what to do and how to do what we had to do. It was *Taaijee* and my *Chachi* who took charge of the pooja at home.

With the help of our close relatives, my brothers performed the last rites. I was too traumatised to see Dad in that crushed state when his body was brought back home. Mom kept asking me to look at him for the last time, but I could not muster the courage.

11. Redeeming myself

Our lives seemed to have come to a halt by the end of 2004. I wasn't working and was out of job, but both my brothers were getting on with their careers. Our relatives believed that Dad had left us cash rich because he earned well and lived well. However, we as a family, knew that Dad did not have savings. His generosity had meant that he would give away money to those who asked and never asked to return. And most of them were his brothers, sisters and friends and their children.

He had not got any life insurance done either. Dad would say that his children were his insurance policy. We were going through the most difficult phase of our lives. Suddenly, after this incident, all three of us matured. As a family we would agree on most matters and had the same values. Bunty was stationed in Chennai on a project and Babloo went on for his course to Kolkata which he had to leave apparently amidst the tragedy.

Mom, Chikki and I were left behind in our house in Gurgaon. Chikki was hardly four years old and remembers very little about his *Nanu*. But as is our tradition, we talk about him, and my son remembers his grandfather on his birthday and wishes all of us.

After Dad passed away, I realised that I would have to earn. It was not a good idea to be overly dependent on my brothers, as dutiful as they were. My parents had supported me in my time of emotional and financial need, and now it was my turn.

Mom started spending more time with Chikki. She said that he was her responsibility, and she would bring him up as her fourth child. I discussed my own role with her, about getting into a career.

We would talk about matters for a long time. As she comes from the old school of thought, she felt that the profession of teaching was respectable and the best option for me. She was wary of anything else, mentioning my standing as a divorcee in society etc. My masters' form had not only been successful, but by this time, I was a Postgraduate in Literature. It enhanced my Graduation and the certificate course in Computer Sciences.

I was glad of a job offer in another well-known school in Dwarka, Delhi and began to teach. Chikki had outgrown play school and was admitted to the same school where I was teaching. I could get us to the school in Dwarka and back home in my car. My day was again structured as I worked hard to prove myself. As I got busy with work, I slowly started coming out of my depression.

The school was a new era school, air-conditioned and with a large auditorium and swimming pool. The assembly grounds were huge and there was a separate basketball field. When my brothers saw the school, they approved and said that this was right for Chikki. I had no second thoughts either.

I got down to it and not only taught but also involved myself in the school activities. I took up coordination for annual functions. It included the involvement of Spic Macay, the Society for Promotion of Indian Classical Music and Culture Amongst Youth. They were also involved in meditation, crafts and any notable aspects of Indian culture for young people.

I was given the responsibility of handling events end-to-end. It included escorting guests till they left, and everything in between. The first event featured Raja and Radha Reddy, exponents of the Kuchipudi dance form and recipients of Padma Shri and Padma Bhushan awards. I felt privileged in their company.

I started loving my job. I wished to be lost in the crowd so that I get very little time to be alone and think. The school Principal and founder at the time, "Veena Raizada" fully approved my suggestions. Given to classical good looks, she came from a strong academic and cultural background herself. I knew I was under her scrutiny in respect of my own hard work, knowledge and information, all of which received compliments from her.

The outcome was that I was allotted additional responsibilities for managing administrative and examination function for the senior wing. It was Ms Raizada who opened my eyes to the possibilities that included counselling as a career option or getting into administrative function. But I had started to like what I was doing.

But as it happens, matters changed to my disadvantage.

Ms Raizada chose other career options and decided to part ways with the school. I was devastated, as I was very close to her. My role in school and my performance would now be scrutinised in a different light and I felt my motivation slipping away. The new Principal had a different outlook and she and I viewed matters of importance quite differently.

Her interactions with me came to a head. I was no longer a highly motivated individual, but became defensive, losing the respect of those whose standing I had once valued. I had not experienced such a situation, so I put in my papers and exited the toxic atmosphere.

Chikki, however, was still doing well and continued in the same school. There was no school bus from Dwarka to Gurgaon, so I continued to drive over 30-minutes to a bus pick-up point and another 30-minutes back, no matter the weather or the time. The bus timing was 6.40 in the morning. It meant we had to leave home by 6.00 am when dawn was breaking. The bus driver and the bus conductor are among the many who rose in my esteem and who I will always remember as those who helped others along the way. They would wait for us if they reached Chikki's pick-up spot and realised that I was about to reach.

Chikki had always been a darling - completing his homework the evening before, waking up at 5.00 in the morning to get ready for school without any hassles, wishing me good morning with a kiss and his smile. Till today, the ritual continues with a morning kiss, and I would have it no other way. I owe everything to God for blessing me, for letting me be his "Pinkoo", as fondly he addresses me. I always feel that he is a favour granted to me by God on account of my disturbed marriage. I have started to count the positives in everything. I felt loved and could deal with any troubles as long as I had my son, Mom and my brothers.

I was jobless, yet again. I wasn't doing anything apart from dropping and picking up Chikki from his pick-up point. One day as I was driving back home after dropping Chikki at the bus stop, I passed a woman who looked familiar. She was with two children at a school bus stop, probably waiting for their bus. I got a glimpse of her as I drove past and wondered who she was. I knew she was someone I had known.

The next day, after dropping Chikki, I thought of halting at the spot where I had seen her. She came along with her children, and I realised that this was my old best friend Sunita! We hugged each other tightly and she took me to her place nearby, which was hardly five minutes from where we met. We were meeting after a gap of eight years and there was a lot to talk about. She started asking about how I had identified her.

I replied, "*dil ki aankhon se*".

She retorted, "very filmy". And we began giggling.

Sunita gave me all her news and I gave her mine. Ironical as it was, we had even more in common because we had had similar marital woes and had moved back to our parental homes.

She was working as a Software Engineer in an insurance company in Cyber City, in Gurgaon. Since we had found each other early in the morning, we had time before she had to leave for work. We started meeting every day, after that. It took us back to our long discussions in the park over *chai* and *samosas*. This time, it was *chai* and *poha* (another popular Indian snack) made and brought by her as we sat in my parked car.

She had to reach office at ten every morning and we would meet around seven. She utilised her breakfast time with me in the car to save time over her own breakfast at home! The way in which I worked it out was to give her a missed call as I was cashless and Sunita called me back. Sunita never ignored my calls and neither did she ever questioned on those missed calls.

I was back to worrying on another count. Nearly four months had passed, and I was still jobless. My brush with the school had left a sour taste and I did not want to go back to school-related work.

I saw Sunita and my brothers happy in their organised corporate jobs and decided to try my luck in that world.

One day while we were discussing my future, I decided to buy a laptop so it would be easier for me to look for jobs. But I had little money, except for one Fixed Deposit in a bank which I had kept for the future. I thought I should encash it as I needed it now rather than later.

I took Sunita along with me to the bank, withdrew the FD that I had and bought my first ever laptop. I also got an internet connection installed at home and started applying for jobs.

The decision of breaking the FD proved fruitful.

Apart from surfing for jobs on my laptop, I also utilised my time looking for contacts through Orkut. It was a social networking service, owned and operated by Google at that time. The service was designed to help users meet friends and maintain existing relationships on social media. In a way, it was the Facebook of our times.

It helped me to find my friend and mentor at NIIT, Anjali. She had risen to the top in her selected field and was the Managing Director of her own placement agency. We were ecstatic as we talked on Orkut. I counted my blessings. Once again, I was getting my loved ones back into my life. I had Mom and Chikki, Sunita and Anjali here in Gurgaon!

Anjali did me the favour of providing me with a long-awaited job break. Some nine months after I'd left the school, I joined her as a Team Leader for her recruitment team. I had no experience in the domain, but Anjali guided and trained me. Its very important to have a mentor in your life and I was fortunate to have her. As a recruiter, I got the experience of working on the "Naukri" platform, one of the major job boards in India, and was no longer a job seeker, rather was now finding jobs for others!

Pretty exciting!!

Simultaneously, I got myself enrolled for evening classes for a two-year course in Human Resource Management at Amity University.

After having served the consultancy for almost an year, I got my first corporate job at "Skipper Electricals". The organisation was a heavy engineering manufacturer, with distribution and power generation in over 50 countries. I was the first HR person on-boarded under the leadership of the then CEO, Commodore Rakesh Sardana, who is amongst the best of my many bosses.

Commodore Sardana was an IIT graduate who had retired from the Indian Navy. He was a straight-talking man who had come directly into this corporate job after his retirement. I had found a supportive mentor again, in a totally different sector. I learned a lot in my two years association with him.

The company often participated in ELECRAMA, the platform to connect the world with the Indian industry in respect of technology, with future energy transition included. It was at an exhibition in Mumbai, amidst industrial conglomerates and a buzz of exciting new things to come, I was dazzled to see how big the world of corporates is. My eyes opened to whole new world of possibilities, and I decided to make my next move.

Everything was going smoothly, but as the saying goes "We need to challenge ourselves to see a better version of ourselves". I never wanted to be in a comfortable situation. I wasn't born to have an easy life. I had different aspirations which I could foresee would not be met in this company. I had spent close to two years in the organization and learned much.

My ambitions were fuelled. I was seeking for an organization which required pure HR sans an administrative function role.

I was thrilled to find the kind of organisation and the managerial infrastructure I had been looking for in another engineering conglomerate "Continental Engines". I underwent four strenuous interview rounds with the panel before being placed as Manager, Corporate HR.

I could fit in better with the time I needed to drop Chikki off to the pick-up spot for his school bus. The arrangement was that in the morning I would drop Chikki and Mom would pick him up at the end of his school day in the afternoon. She said she enjoyed it and did not complain even though she was getting on in years.

At this stage I could definitely say that my life had been a circle of events. The best of people came back, I loved to be able to be with Chikki and the skills that I had learned would never be wasted. Mom's driving skills returned over the eight to ten years during which she picked up Chikki in the afternoon. She said it reminded her of the time when we as children had been in school and she spent much of the time in taking us to where we had to go in that old Ambassador car!

My coming back home to stay with her was a blessing, else she would have been totally on her own.

She had always wanted me and RG to stay together irrespective of my miserable married life. It was also true that Mom and I were strong personalities possibly because we never had any other option except to be strong. Now we were more like argumentative siblings and were known to clash with each other. After all, we did have separate outlooks towards life. Mom would have different notions and I could not change her opinions, no matter how many alternative schools of thought I presented her with.

Perhaps I am still fighting for my freedom. Perhaps someday, I might be able to make her realise that love does not mean control, that if I don't do something the way she wants, it does not mean that I disrespect her and do not love her.

I did get some excellent job opportunities outside Gurgaon, but I wanted to utilise the time with the family which would otherwise be wasted on commuting. For me, being with family is the most important thing in my life. I say this with conviction even though I had shed another family a long time ago that I could never belong to.

12. Exploring and Powering Up

I wanted to reward myself with an overseas trip and wanted a break before I started my new journey. I had a hard time convincing Mom to let me and Chikki travel alone. After lengthy discussions, Mom agreed to let us fly to the nearest holiday destination abroad – "Dubai".

Chikki and I took off for a week, stayed at the "Burj-al-Arab", billed as Dubai's most iconic hotel, it definitely was to us. We had not only looked for luxury but had also added to the best when we booked a suite overlooking the sea. I splurged on the trip and opted for the most interesting itinerary offered by the travel agent.

We went on a dinner cruise and desert safari. We also visited the mall in Burj Khalifa, and I felt like a tiny ant amidst the grandeur of Dubai.

I instinctively connect with the culture of different places and the people I meet there. So far, the main cities that I had been travelling to in adulthood were Mumbai and Jaipur. I lived in an area that had once been replete with heritage.

Dubai had a heritage and culture of its own, with the intersection of a great many cultures. Then, there was the shopping. We shopped to our heart's content and managed to have a great time before we came home to Gurgaon and to my new job.

I immersed myself into my new job, managing my work, family time and family expenses better. The company was well known in the field of design, development and manufacture of critical automotive components. The Chairman's second pet project was a real estate venture. Their prime development was Central Park on the Golf course road and Sohna road in Gurgaon.

The corporate office was located at the Global Business Park building in Gurgaon and was spread over an entire floor. On account of the 2000 full time employees and 500 odd contractual staff, the HR function was not only major but well-structured and streamlined.

I eased into corporate HR, handling recruitment for the Assistant General Manager level and above for their component business, and at all levels of the vehicles business. Keshav Pathak, Head of HR was striking in looks and personality. He was extremely disciplined, arriving long before the regular office time in order to catch up on his day. He was an early bird and would show up at 8.00 in the morning. I always looked for excuses to speak with him as he had insights into the evolving human resource function. I figured that the best time to catch him was before 9:30 am.

I was in awe of Mr Pathak and would try to emulate his example by reaching office before time to ask for his opinion on job related matters. I also wanted to know his opinion on what human resources meant in this organisation.

I learnt a lot, because the meetings with Mr Pathak were better than reading about our functions in a textbook. Besides the professional framework, I sought guidance from him on how to up-skill further. I was impressed by his depth and width of knowledge and can easily claim that he takes the numero uno position among professionals that I have met during my career. "A thorough professional with no strings attached".

The company was struggling to make revenues from its vehicle business. The vision was to surpass the major competitors in the 3-wheeler business. Colleagues here were cooperative, and I was required to visit the vehicles and components plants, both out-of-town, albeit on long drives. The then COO "Yogesh Sharma" and "Anoop Gupta" would give me a lift by turn to Bhiwadi to the auto components plant, while "Tejveer Sidana", CEO, helped me get to Roorkee, where the vehicles were manufactured. I visited both the hubs once every two months. I was lucky to have met these professionals who were very cooperative and knowledgeable and later went on to becoming my best buddies.

One of the friends at Continental was "Amit Dixit", Head of the IT function. He oversaw the concern and its subsidiary for his department. Initially he found me rude and arrogant, and we hardly spoke to each other during the first year of my joining at Conti (as Continental was internally referred). Once his team member resigned and I was given the assignment to coordinate and help him find the right talent for the role. That is when we started bonding over the interviews, meetings, discussions and various other official matters.

He had started to bald early but was dynamic and we got along well, enough to walk and chat after lunch on the ground floor of the tower. Amit and I spoke about home and personal matters, rather than professional ones, as with Keshav Pathak. My HR hat helped to keep a distance and a demarcation. His perception of me changed completely when we started chatting. We would often go for lunches together and discuss life as a mystery. We could speak and discuss on any subject, such was the comfort level I had with him. Funnily though, he wished to be addressed as Shree Shree Amit Dixit Jee, just to feel respected.

One day while chatting on different aspects of life, I asked him "Why do relationships break?" I knew that Amit would have a novel answer.

He did, when he said, "Every relationship has a time period. Once its purpose is over, we meet new people in our lives".

That hit me really hard. But I learnt and had to move on when ironically, this would be true for our friendship too. He introduced me to his beautiful wife, and we became good friends, but something somewhere didn't click.

About the organisation, I concluded that Indian businesses, however well thought of and successfully run, had many strata of personnel. I found out that there were eyes of the owners spread throughout and at all levels of the engineering firm. In a sense, this was both, a strength and a weakness. It provided the topmost echelon with a great deal of unsubstantiated gossip, some of which could no doubt be useful to them.

Dealing with personnel at such informal levels was also dangerous. However, it was a challenge, as the company was not ready to introspect with regards to its authoritarian leadership. The leader would impose his expectations and define the outcomes he expected. As

I knew it, a one-person show could only be successful in situations when a leader is the most knowledgeable in the team.

However, though this is an efficient strategy in time-constrained periods, creativity is bound to be sacrificed since input from a team operating under such a leader is limited. There was suspicion all around and personnel took time to watch their own backs. The downside was that the practice is bound to lead to rebellion amongst bosses and their team members. And that was what happened.

Mr Pathak wanted to retire and was looking for a replacement for himself. That didn't go well with me, since I had fitted in well with the people I was working with. Him finding a replacement was not a challenge, reporting to someone else was, to me. Finally, he found someone, and the person came on board. The new boss was very different and not a patch on Mr Pathak. I work with people and not organizations. I was emotionally invested in people working there but I could foresee that I will not step up in my learning curve here, I decided to end my journey. And with the change in job, it was also the end of my friendship with Amit for obvious reasons.

A trio never works!!

13. महफ़िल में तेरी हम न रहें जो, गम तो नहीं है, गम तो नहीं है।

We meet people in our lives with whom we can develop great relationships because of shared interests, common social circles or some blood connection. But beyond these common reasons are those relationships that are the product of a more spiritual and intimate connection.

Such a connection, whether platonic or romantic, transcends the practical details that holds together other relationships. Such relationships are rare and not easy to come across. Soul connections are profound in ways that are beyond physical attraction or someone's charm. One cannot explain what such a connection is; it must be experienced to be understood. I had such a relationship with "Prabhas", not to be confused with the Tollywood actor of the magnum opus "Bahubali" series.

Prabhas was introduced to me via a colleague at Conti and the connect was instant. He not only worked elsewhere but was also in another city thousands of kilometres away from me. Initially we didn't get the chance to see each other and communicated via our cell phones, but I could sense from the start that our souls had connected and that it was special.

Regarding the first time I saw him, I can safely say that he was akin to my ideal man, the hero of my teenaged Mills & Boon novels - tall, dark and handsome. We might have been soul connects and recognised this in each other. He was my best friend and more. One person who knew me more than anyone else. But sadly, no matter how strong the bond between us, something somewhere did not click and even today I am still trying to figure out what went wrong and where.

We struggled to understand each other. Miscommunication was common throughout our time together. We would argue about petty matters, and I could not fathom where I stood with him. I found it difficult to read his signals. The disagreements would quickly get personal and move swiftly from one subject to another, negating the original point. Apart from communication, the other important factor that was missing in our relation was comprehension. We always kept arguing on who is right, and did not give much thought to what exactly the other was wanting to say, failing to comprehend the actual zest of the discussions.

More so during that time, I was at my worst with my life's experiences, and at the same time most vulnerable. I tried hard to explain but he couldn't understand that it wouldn't be an easy relationship for me. I had developed this bad habit of overthinking, tended to overreact more than I should have. And I would get insecure and demanded reassurance occasionally. This was something he couldn't handle as he failed to understand the reason why I was like that. It ended with the same speed as it started.

However, his charismatic personality and values had a great impact on my transformation. We may have had our share of arguments over our difference of opinions, but one thing appreciative about him was that he had a respectful outlook towards women. He always tried to help me see both sides of the coins, and even to look for a third side before entering into any argument. His learnings were deep.

He was one personality with whom I have experienced the Karmic connection. On a spiritual level I am a firm believer of Karma and Karmic relationships. "A Karmic relationship is one that can be filled with all-consuming passion but is extremely difficult to maintain. We get into the Karmic dynamic because we have to learn to love and respect ourselves," is the axiom for me.

Others may consider it to be a controversial perspective, applicable in some cases to bad relationships with a silver lining that we are somehow destined to be in.

I have more Pundits to quote. "Karmic relationships are love lessons," explains Bonnie Winston. "They can be as fulfilling and monumental as long-term partnerships. However, not all relationships are meant to be happily ever after."

Also, as Carrie Bradshaw said in Sex and the City, "Some loves aren't epic novels; some are short stories, but that doesn't make them any less filled with love and learning." Mine may not be an epic novel, it's definitely my favourite.

While there are many negatives to a Karmic relationship, Winston explains that their purpose is to teach us something new. "They are tutorials for our souls to hopefully become better people and correct past hurts", which I can now see the sense of.

With this relationship I learnt to love myself, I became more compassionate and humbler. Today I can confidently say that I am at peace with "everyone" in my life, that I am able to judge the scale of an issue and do not show anger if I deem it to be trivial.

This relationship, failed or not, has taught me to be respectful and loving towards every individual and I am indebted to it. My objective now is to continue to be self-aware as I carry on by finding satisfaction at work, at home and to think of friends old and new with affection.

In a sense, Prabhas entered my life and coached me. I went with the flow. The person I am now, strong, confident, and at the same time empathetic, I can attribute to him. Prabhas has a place in my life and a special role in my coming back to life. If it was understanding on the subject of love, for me the understanding came from Prabhas. I have no qualms that I didn't get the love I thought I deserved, but I know today what the true essence of love is.

You can call it a form of transmutation for me. He showed me what my life ahead might be like, whether on my own or with friends and family.

I think about the woman I was and the woman I have become. I think about how much I always wanted to be this person and live life on my terms - earning for my family, loving the work that I do, people who care about me and whose opinion I will always value. I was not always like this, it was Prabhas who gave me the insight to view other people and my world in this light.

From Amit I learnt the true essence of friendship and with Prabhas I encountered the true definition of love. Both played a great role in my life. Others have stabbed me in my back, and some have stood by me during my worst times, while some have left me when I needed them the most, and some hated me. Irrespective of how I was treated in any relationship or friendship, I can claim that I have always been very true. I have also learnt to accept flaws – in others and most importantly in myself.

14. Having the Thames of my life

I found, contacted and grabbed an offer from a multinational bio-pharma consulting firm "Prescient Healthcare Group Pvt Ltd". Its corporate office is in London and most of the clients are in Europe and The United States of America.

I was to get onboarded in the organization in August of 2017, but before that, as I have made a ritual for myself, I gave myself another treat of exploring other parts of the world. I realised that a break between two jobs is very important because it helps you to relax and enjoy yourself before plunging into a new job.

Starting a new job is exciting, but it can still be a challenging big life change. You are likely to have a new schedule, commute, work culture and job duties to get used to. In order to not compare your present with your past, a break is a must to unlearn some past experiences and make space for new ones.

I had an offer from my youngest brother Bunty for a holiday with him and his family in London, no less.

So, this time I travelled to the UK. First Dubai, and now this! It was an opportunity to sample other lands and travel to far off destinations. I was going to the UK where Bunty and his family were currently stationed. Bunty's career had taken off and he was posted to London with his wife and his little munchkin, Keenya.

I will not dwell on what I consider past failures, and a departure from friends and acquaintances whom I liked as I took to planning this holiday for Chikki and myself.

I found out the history of London, got to see the sights I had only seen on picture postcards and read about. As a student of Literature and what has been documented by our colonial rulers, I had some knowledge about their culture.

Chikki, Mom and I talked long and hard about the number of opportunities that were landing on my plate. First the job offer and now this from Bunty and his wife Hina! Bunty also said that he was happy to sponsor me. I was determined to make the best of it, and so was Chikki. We soaked up the thrill of it all.

We travelled to England during the glorious summer of 2017.

Both Chikki and I were equally excited. We stayed three whole weeks. Chikki was beside himself with the thought of adventure because he had another must-see, must-do ask. As a great fan of football and Manchester United in particular, he also had an eye on Manchester and a visit to the club grounds at Old Trafford. Chikki said it was his and Bobby Charlton's 'Theatre of Dreams'.

And so, it would not only be London that we would target. We decided and planned over and over, took advice and took off from the Indira Gandhi Airport in Delhi to Heathrow Airport in England. Chikki and I seemed to have been dreaming for too long and too hard, with the result that our other-worldliness led to a funny incident at the Heathrow luggage collection belt.

Chikki picked up someone else's similar looking suitcase and I did not notice either. We realised our mistake when we got to Bunty's, because the clothes were definitely not ours. As protocol and another effort, we made the switch the next morning to return the suitcase to the airlines and pick up ours. Now we could begin as we had planned.

Would I get to see the world icon Big Ben? I pinched myself when I did. Was I really looking at what I thought I was? I managed to convince myself that I really was. We spent the day visiting Buckingham Palace, Trafalgar Square, Westminster Abbey and Madame Tussaud's. We made time for the London Eye — the Millennium Wheel, the cantilevered observation wheel on the South Bank of the River Thames.

At first look the London Eye resembled a giant's spoked bicycle wheel and took me back to the bicycle I rode to school and back every day. Its capsules were the 'eyes' as it afforded an eagle eye view of much of what is picture perfect London from some height up above the city.

Our minds were awhirl with the many sights and sounds of what used to be London town. We partook of the local food (a little too bland), and took note of the fast pace of the city. Much of our own pace was enabled by the London tube, the underground railway started over a hundred years ago, in 1890! That weekend wc also experienced the big red London buses and the tube of lore, but found that there were so many interesting spots to hop off at, that it was impossible to see the entire city despite having three weeks on our hands.

There was another big city waiting for us, mostly for Chikki. We took the train with Bunty and family, over-ground this time. My brother and sister-in-law were with us, and I could see that determined yet dreamy look on Chikki's face as we headed for the Old Trafford. The two guys…Bunty and Chikki went ahead for a stadium tour.

Hina and I, along with Keenya had planned a different kind of expedition. We shopped at the Trafford Centre, savoured the shopping buzz in what looked like a city by itself and was thronged with people.

One drawback was the incessant English rain. It was cold that afternoon and limited our time there. We got back to a tad warmer London and to Bunty's cosy flat. London was where we were to live through for the rest of our holiday.

Soon, too soon, three weeks passed by. When the time came to depart, it was hard to say goodbye to our family in London and to this beautiful city. The memories remain as England has been amongst the best of trips for Chikki and me.

We arrived back at the Indira Gandhi International Airport and made it to our home. Mom was there, a few more grey hairs added as she worried about us and wreathed in smiles to welcome us back. I made a resolution to try to explain to her not only the wonderful holiday that we had had, but also the new me after that experience.

15. Reflections

I got to my work place a couple of days after my return from England, with renewed vigour. My role at Prescient, was being accountable for the Human resource function. I got onboarded as the Head of Talent & Performance Management.

At first, I prided myself for the many sectors in which I had picked up experience - education, heavy engineering, EPC, automotive and now healthcare. Ironically, a few months into the job, I was faced with challenges which at first, I thought had floored me. Was I thinking too soon?

At Prescient, the work culture, its people and a whole new professional world was quite different for me from what I had come across elsewhere in my career. At that point of time, I felt it might be too much for me to handle. Was I cut out for a new kind of professionalism despite my degrees and certificates? Initially it felt like a let-down. I just hoped I would not be too disappointed with myself to end up in crying and having sleepless nights again. I was beginning to feel terrible.

My brothers supported and counselled me in this time of confusion by encouraging me to own my decision. They said, "think about the people who would love to see you fail" and asked me if I would want to give them that pleasure.

My mind responded, "Do not rest on your laurels, Anamika. Some day you will look back and be glad that you did not give up".

"No", I replied with confidence, "I could not give up, ever".

My own mantra helped me in this situation too - step back from the problem and analyse it from a distance!

I have lived through many difficulties but have always found my way on my own. I can say that at times I fell, then got up, ran, fell again and got up again. Every time I fell, I would look up and talk to God. I would meditate and converse with him in my thoughts, "So this is the new exam you have planned for me? Fine, let me find the solution. I too want to see for how long you have oceans of problems for me". God was my best friend, always smiling and saying, "Keep going, this is life, I am with you".

And I would say, "It's alright God, if you say so. I trust you".

I was a case study for myself because that is what worked. I bounced back with renewed energy, focus and enthusiasm. What started as a difficult proposition initially which I was willing to give up, turned into a transformational journey for myself. I began to look forward to the next day at work...and the next...and the next... and I shall be hitting on my first milestone of five years at Prescient by August 2022.

I can't grab all the credit for my renewed determination at Prescient. "Swati" who is President and Managing

Director, "Rakesh", President and Head of Intelligence & Insight Business and "Victoria": Chief Talent Officer, along with the other stalwarts of the leadership team, were more open-minded, politely honest and supportive than any of the other corporates I have worked in. They helped me along the way.

Yes, as in any corporate profile, criticism is evident. In fact, criticism of any kind can be hard to swallow, especially when it comes to something you spent time and energy on. Inherently, we all want to do a good job. But criticism is just as important as praise, if not more so. Good, constructive feedback can help you improve and guide you towards new heights you might not have achieved otherwise. Swati kept fuelling in me the urge to be better with each passing day, providing me with constructing feedbacks at regular intervals and I too accepted them graciously.

Rakesh filled in for Swati when she had to go for her maternity leaves. I had the chance to work with him in Swati's absence. He was a delight to work with. The charismatic smile never faded from his face, irrespective of how strenuously occupied he was considering the dual responsibilities he was handling that time. His quick tips on leadership from his own experience have stayed with me. I even received the Spot Award from him, which was an honour, especially considering the short timespan that we worked together. I also keep the said award on my work desk, it is a constant reminder for me to keep moving forward and performing better in my work.

Victoria's motivating statement in her famous British accent, "C'mon, you can do it. Go for it", has always inspired me to endeavour tasks which ideally

I wouldn't. Whenever I get stuck, these lines echo in my head, encouraging me to pursue and finish tasks which initially seem difficult. Today, I can say that I am thrilled to be part of such a vibrant team.

In my life's journey, I have come across strong women like my Mom, Hina, Sunita, Varsha, Swati and Victoria and all these brilliant women are different from each other, yet they have impacted my life in a way that if given a chance I would like to see them heading different ministries of our government - They will do wonders, I am sure!!

A few years into my organisation, I underwent TMSDI, England. TMS Development International (TMSDI) offers learning and development professionals a unique approach to personal, team and organisational performance. This is a work preferences diagnostic tool that is designed to help people understand how they prefer to communicate, what types of work they prefer to do and how they make decisions in a work environment. That there are no right or wrong answers, the profile looks at work preferences only and not at skills or capabilities.

The course helped me to have a deeper sense of personalities and their preferred choices. Most importantly, it cleared my definition of introverts vs extroverts. It helped me to realise that being introvert is my preference and I should not see it as an hinderance.

Since childhood I was an introvert. I did a good lot of reading and can today say with conviction that brilliant human beings like Albert Einstein, Steven Spielberg, Isaac Newton, Marc Zuckerberg, Elon Musk, Hillary Clinton and my all-time favourite... Barack Obama, are all deep thinking, introverted personalities.

Yes, I should not have wasted my energies by trying to force myself to be someone else. My life or work roles did not require it. What I could do was up-skill myself further in my domain in Human Resources and that is not only the best thought, but it is also right for me. I have learnt much and am still learning.

As of today March 2022, I have realised that we have lived through nearly two years of the Covid pandemic. During this time, the entire world worked from home, and the firm I work for was no exception. Me and my colleagues were provided with infrastructure and the flexibility as we settled down to this new 'work from home' culture.

These two years have been the best in terms of learning, introspection and spending time with my family and I consider myself to be a blessed soul. Best of all, I no longer regret my past ruinous experiences. Despite two deadly waves of the pandemic there are very few options of travel and going out, but for me, the pandemic has been bliss.

Considering my past experiences with my friendships and relationships, it was hard to make friends and difficult to be at ease in large gatherings. Even now, I avoid large scale functions, but that is for other reasons and not about questioning myself or those I would like to be friendly with.

This memoir of mine has been a mix of intergenerational members of my family and friends. As for those who are most special to me, they possess an other-worldly godliness. I have been oriented into my North-West Indian grid with my beliefs and religious rituals intact. I'm not fearful anymore and do not have any hatred feeling for any one I have come across irrespective of how unpleasant their behaviour was. I pass on my blessings to them!!

I'm thoroughly satisfied with every decision I have made. I'm happiest with the one child I have been blessed with. He is doing wonders in his engineering course and has plans to pursue Masters. He gives me strength and makes this world a better place for me to inhabit. "What is awesomely overwhelming is that he never forgets to greet me every year on Father's Day. As a mother, I wonder what special I have done to be graced with such a special gift, altogether treasured. I am blessed. What more could I ask for?"

Yes, for me as a single woman, life is no longer a puzzle with missing pieces. It has been an independent journey. However, it is not that I no longer desire the comfort of a companionship, but I am contemplating if it's worth giving up on freedom and independence by compromising my individuality. Sometimes I miss the silence that I would probably want to share with someone special, but now having been independent and single for almost two decades, I love and cherish "my own company" and "me time" to an extent that the mere idea of someone entering my territory, give me heebie-jeebies.

I have discovered the joys of being self-reliant. I love to make my bed in my own way, follow a certain rule in my kitchen, have my own schedules for the day and a regular regime for the night.

My journey has been an empowering route of self-discovery. I have set myself free from the bond. Love, to me now means Lord *Krishna*!

I analysed my hurts and put them to rest, found my strengths, rediscovered myself and moved on.

The journey isn't over yet, I am enroute to embark on the untouched interesting incidents in my forthcoming phase of life.

समझनी है ज़िन्दगी तो पीछे देखो, जीनी है ज़िन्दगी तो आगे देखो